THE MAN
WHO NEVER WAS

BY EWEN MONTAGU

With a foreword by LORD ISMAY, G.C.B., C.H., D.S.O.

SCHOLASTIC BOOK SERVICES
NEW YORK•TORONTO•LONDON•AUCKLAND•SYDNEY•TOKYO

TO THE TEAM

Copyright 1953 by Walter Louis D'Arcy Hart and Oliver Harry Frost. This edition is published by Scholastic Book Services, a division of Scholastic Magazines, Inc., by arrangement with J. B. Lippincott Company.

22 21 20 19 18 17 16 15 14 13 12 11   7 8 9/7 01/8

Printed in the U.S.A.

Foreword

To MYSTIFY and mislead the enemy has always
been one of the cardinal principles of war. Consequently, *ruses de guerre* of one kind or another
have played a part in almost every campaign ever
since the episode of the Trojan horse, or perhaps
even earlier.

The game has been played for so long that it is
not easy to think out new methods of disguising one's
strength or one's intentions. Moreover, meticulous
care must be exercised in the planning and execution
of these schemes. Otherwise, so far from deceiving
the enemy, they merely give the show away.

The Allies decided that their next step, after the
battle for Tunisia, should be the invasion of Italy
through Sicily. We felt sure—one always does on
these occasions—that this was such an obvious cor-
ollary to the North African campaign, that the
enemy would expect it and concentrate to meet it.
What could be done to put them off the scent?

I so well remember how I was brought, one evening, the outlines of a cover plan which was ulti-
mately given the somewhat gruesome name of
"Operation Mincemeat." I was, I confess, a little

dubious whether it would work; but I put it up to
the Chiefs of Staff, who approved it in principle.
Thereafter, Lieutenant-Commander Montagu, who
originated the idea, and his colleagues went full
steam ahead.

The operation succeeded beyond our wildest
dreams. To have spread-eagled the German defensive effort right across Europe, even to the extent
of sending German vessels away from Sicily itself,
was a remarkable achievement. Those who landed in
Sicily, as well as their families, have cause to be
especially grateful.

It is not often that the whole story of a secret
operation can be made public, told by someone who
knows every detail. The military student can be
grateful that chance has made it possible for him to
have a text-book example of a very specialised
branch of the art of war: others will enjoy a "real-
life thriller"—which once more illustrates that truth
is stranger than fiction.

General the Rt. Hon. LORD ISMAY,
G.C.B., C.H., D.S.O.
*former Secretary-General of the North Atlantic
Treaty Organization and, from 1940 to 1946,
Chief of Staff to Mr. Winston Churchill, the
Minister of Defense.*
Paris.
7th June, 1953

Author's Note

THIS IS A TRUE ACCOUNT of an Operation carried out in the years 1942-1943. Such facts as are not within my own personal knowledge are derived from contemporary documents and reports, and are neither based on anyone's recollection of what happened ten years ago nor on anyone's attempts to justify his actions or those of his associates.

I naturally could not speak or write about it until a fictional story partially based on this operation, and references in German memoirs to the receipt of the documents which formed the basis of this deception, made it clear that it would no longer be possible to maintain that secrecy which all of us who took part in the operation had preserved. This fact was recognised by the authorities, who doubtless appreciated the possible dangers and disadvantages which might result from publication by partially informed writers, and I was given official permission to publish the full story.

The operation was carried out by a team who must, unfortunately, remain anonymous as some of them are still in Government service, therefore I have substituted a false Christian name for

"George's" real one; I have also, of course, maintained the secrecy of "Major Martin's" identity. Where I have referred to other persons I have used the titles and ranks that they held at the time of the operation.

If anyone studies this story, some good may result. Perhaps, when some "leakage" of a secret document is reported, the public may not be so ready as they have been to blame our security services; they may wonder whether the security services have been stupid—or clever?

I must record my thanks to Lord Ismay for his help in 1942 and 1943 and for writing the Foreword, as well as to Jack Garbutt of the *Sunday Express* for his great kindness and for the wise advice which he gave me on this, my first, excursion into authorship.

I wish to acknowledge my deep indebtedness to all my colleagues, without whose loyal help and brilliant inventiveness there could have been no "Operation Mincemeat." And also my indebtedness to Viscount Norwich, without whose unwitting assistance there could have been no publication of this story.

EWEN MONTAGU.

Warren Beach,
Beaulieu.
1953.

CONTENTS

1. The Birth of an Idea 1
2. Preliminary Inquiries 11
3. "Operation Mincemeat" 17
4. The Vital Document 29
5. Major Martin, Royal Marines 44
6. The Creation of a Person 61
7. Major Martin Gets Ready for War 76
8. The Journey North 85
9. The Launching of the Body 90
10. Major Martin Lands in Spain 99
11. We Tidy Up in England 107
12. The German Intelligence Service Plays Its Part 112
13. The German High Command Gets Busy 129
    Envoi 142
    Appendix I 144
    Appendix II 149

THE
BIRTH
OF
AN
IDEA

IN THE GRAVEYARD of the Spanish town of Huelva there lies a British subject. As he died, alone, in the foggy damp of England in the late autumn of 1942, he little thought that he would lie forever under the sunny skies of Spain after a funeral with full military honors, nor that he would, after death, render a service to the Allies that saved many hundreds of British and American lives. In life he had done little for his country; but in death he did more than most could achieve by a lifetime of service.

It all really started through a wild idea of George's. He and I were members of a small inter-Service and inter-departmental committee which used to meet weekly to deal with questions of the security of intended operations. We exchanged and discussed information that had been obtained from all kinds of sources—from our own Services and other sources at home as well as from neutral countries, together with Intelligence reports from enemy countries. With all this and the latest information as to Allied "intentions"—not only immediate and probable, but also "long-term possible"—we had to try to detect any leakages that might have occurred and any "intelligent anticipation" that the enemy might already have made, and also to guard against such leakages and anticipations in the future.

It was not an easy task, but the committee was a good one: it comprised not only Regular officers of considerable knowledge and experience, but also temporary officers and civilians with most varied backgrounds; we were a mixed lot, and between us we could view any item of information as it would strike observers from any walk of life; we had a thoroughly variegated fund of knowledge and there were few spheres of activity with which we had no contacts.

George produced his idea during a discussion over a report with which we had been supplied from occupied Europe; as happened from time to time, we were puzzled whether it was genuine or had been planted by the Germans for transmission to the Allies.

George had one of those subtle and ingenious minds which is forever throwing up fantastic ideas—mostly so ingenious as either to be impossible of implementation or so intricate as to render their efficacy problematical, but every now and again quite brilliant in their simplicity. As we puzzled whether this particular report was genuine, or whether the Germans had captured the agent concerned and were sending reports through him or for him, George remembered a recent warning that had been issued reminding officers that it was forbidden for secret documents to be carried in aircraft lest they should be shot down in enemy territory.

Starting from that, George suddenly suggested that as a check on such reports we should try to get the Germans to plant something on us that we knew was planted, so that we could see what their line was and how they put it over: if we could drop a resistance workers' wireless set into France (he suggested) and it started working it would be difficult to tell whether the Germans or a friendly Frenchman was working it, but if it dropped accompanied by a dead body attached to a badly opened parachute, the task of checking might be easier. A Frenchman would probably tell us what had occurred, whereas the Germans would be more likely to conceal what had happened and work the set as if the agent was still alive. It would not be certain, but it did not involve much effort and might be worth trying. "Does anyone know whether we can get a body?" asked George.

This was not one of his better inspirations, and we rapidly demolished it; agents did not carry their codes or their routine and system for sending messages with them for anyone to find, so how would the Germans transmit messages?

Also, if a parachute failed, whatever was hanging from it would be bound to hit the ground with a considerable bump; if it was a body, this would almost certainly result in a broken limb as well as grazes and scratches, and injuries inflicted after death can always be detected. There was therefore no hope of dropping a dead body attached to a partially opened parachute without the finder being able to tell that the body had been dead for some time before it hit the ground. Besides, even if we could get a dead body (and no one knew whether we could), our field of choice would indeed be limited if it had to be that of someone who had died through falling from a height! No—this was one of George's failures, and we quickly turned back to our report: was it genuine or not? But some months later George's wild idea produced results.

By the summer of 1942 our little committee was in the midst of its first big job. "Operation Torch," the invasion of North Africa, was being mounted, and the experience that we had gained in trying to guard the security of small-scale operations, involving relatively few units, was receiving its first full test.

In spite of all that could be done in the way of security, it was obviously impossible to prevent the enemy knowing that something was brewing. In the first place, it was apparent to everyone that the Allies would not just sit back indefinitely: there must be an invasion somewhere. Secondly, there could be no restriction on foreign diplomats: they moved around the country and they met and spoke to people, not only people in the know, but also some of the thousands who were bound to see the congregation of ships or of troops before they left this country; and whatever view had to be taken officially, none of us had any illusions as to the neutrality of a number of diplomats. Besides, even a pro-British diplomat had a job to do: he had to report to his Government what was going on over here, and once the report got to his country there could be no doubt that there would be at least one official or minister over there who was either paid, or at any rate ideologically ready, to pass the information on to the Germans. Thirdly, there were neutral businessmen and sailors travelling between this country and the Continent.

Therefore we could not hope to prevent the Germans knowing that there *was* an operation afoot.

What we could hope to do was to prevent the vital information of "When?" and "Where?" leaking.

Until the invasion of North Africa had taken place the Allies had no presumptive foothold on the continent of Europe, and the war in North Africa consisted of a campaign in which we were pushing from east to west with our armies based on the Suez Canal Zone. As a result of this situation there was no reason why the Allies should not make an attack at almost any point. As far as the Germans knew, we might land in Norway, in the Low Countries or in France, or try to push up through Spain; we might seize the Canaries or the Azores to help in the war against U-boats; or we might land in Libya to attack Rommel's army in its rear. Except in Egypt, we were wholly uncommitted, and any place in German-held Europe or neutral countries was open to assault.

In these circumstances all that it was necessary for our committee to try to ensure, when we attacked Dieppe or the Lofoten Islands or planned any other assault, was that the actual target and date did not get over to the enemy. That involved nothing more than leaking a false target to the troops concerned, perhaps backing such leaks up with papers about an issue of sun helmets—if they were in fact going to the Lofoten Islands—or something of that kind, and then working really hard to reduce, as much as possible, the bits of information which would inevitably get out of this country. In other words, our principle was to try to make security as complete as possible, and then try to prevent any leakage that *did* get by our precautions being such as would give away the true target.

When "Operation Torch" was being launched against North Africa we could still operate on this basis and, as we studied our Intelligence reports and learned of the movements that the Germans made, we realized that this system had worked as the potential targets were so many that the Germans could not get a definite idea even of where we would strike.

But our problem would be entirely different after "Operation Torch" had been completed. At that stage of the war the Allies would have command of the whole of the North African coast and would be poised ready to strike at what Prime Minister Churchill called "the soft under-belly of Europe." Our committee was kept in touch with the strategic thinking of our Chiefs of Staff and also with that of the Americans. We knew that there were some differences of opinion, but there was a definite probability that we would strike there, and our committee had to be prepared to play our part when the Allies attacked.

With the whole North African coast in Allied hands it was pretty obvious that we would not turn round and transport all those troops back to England for an invasion of France across the Channel, and at least some of them were bound to be used across the Mediterranean. They could form part of an army for the conquest of Italy or they could be used for landing in the South of France or in Greece. Any one of these campaigns was a possibility, and our committee had to be prepared to deal with whatever might eventually be decided upon. We might perhaps have been able to cope with this task on the system which had worked so well up till then had that been the whole story, but there was one feature of the strategic situation which created a new problem.

Sicily lay in the middle of the Mediterranean like a football at the toe of Italy, and until it had been captured the passing of a convoy through the Mediterranean was a major operation attended by enormous losses, and this situation would remain even when the airfields in North Africa were finally in our hands. It was made clear to our committee that the reduction of Sicily would almost certainly have to be undertaken before any of the other operations could take place. As we always had to make our preparations long before an operation was launched, we were considering this next job, the security of the invasion of Sicily, even before "Torch" was finally mounted.

And here we foresaw trouble. If Sicily was a clear probability to us, once North Africa was in

Allied hands, it would be just as clear a probability to the Germans. Indeed, as the Prime Minister eventually said, when approving this operation of ours, it did not matter taking some risk of revealing Sicily as the target, as "anybody but a damn' fool would *know* it is Sicily." How would we be able, when the time came, to prevent the Germans from reinforcing the defenses of Sicily to a dangerous extent as the result of the same strategic reasoning which had caused the Allies to attack it?

As we were puzzling over this problem, the penny suddenly dropped, and George's fantastic idea of some time before justified itself. "Why," I said, "shouldn't we get a body, disguise it as a staff officer, and give him really high-level papers which will show clearly that we are going to attack somewhere else. We won't have to drop him on land, as the aircraft might have come down in the sea on the way round to the Med. He would float ashore with the papers either in France or in Spain; it won't matter which. Probably Spain would be best, as the Germans wouldn't have as much chance to examine the body there as if they got it into their own hands, while it's certain that they will get the documents, or at least copies." So the idea was born. Excitedly, we discussed its potentialities. We would have to check on a number of points: What sort of condition would a body be in after an aircraft crash in the sea? What were the usual causes of death in such cases? What would a post mortem reveal? Could we get a suitable body—indeed, could we get *any* body? Such were the first questions to which we would have to get answers. If those were satisfactory the plan was worth studying with care, for none of us doubted that, given the chance, the Spaniards would play the part for which we had cast them, and then what a chance we would have given ourselves!

2

PRELIMINARY INQUIRIES

WE HAD TALKED GLIBLY of "getting a body," but we had realized that there would be difficulties; we had yet to learn how difficult it would actually be. None of us, indeed, entirely liked the idea, for even in the stress of war one's natural respect for the sanctity of the human body remains a powerful instinct. But for us that instinct was overborne by a realization of the lives that could be saved by the temporary use of a body that we were confident would eventually receive a proper and decent burial. The difficulty with which we were immediately faced was that imposed by security. How could we go to relatives in their hour of sorrow and ask to be allowed to take without explanation the remains of the son or husband or brother whom they mourned? And if we had to explain, what could we say? In fiction one could, perhaps, expect that we

would meet a man who happened to be the sole
relative of someone who had just died a death suitable for our plan—a man of that rare type who
would just agree to our taking the body and would
ask no questions as to why we wanted it. In fiction,
perhaps, but not in real life!

Before we started our search, we had first to
make sure what kind of body we needed. If the
Germans were to accept the body as that of the victim of an aircraft crash at sea, we would have to
present them with someone whose body did not
afford signs of a cause of death inconsistent with
that.

It seemed to me that the best approach to this
question would be from the point of view of the
man who would do the post mortem. What would
a pathologist expect to find and what would he expect not to find in the body of a man who had
drifted ashore after an aircraft had been lost at sea?
For, after all, the aircraft need not have actually
crashed.

My thoughts at once turned to Sir Bernard Spilsbury. No one had more experience of pathology
than he had, and I felt that no better security risk
existed: one could be certain that he at any rate
would not gossip or even pass what I said to him
on "in confidence to someone whom he could trust."
In this respect, there had never been any difference
between Sir Bernard and an oyster. And he had one

even rarer quality: I felt sure that he would not
ask any questions other than those needed for the
solution of the problem put to him: *he* would just
take the fact that we wanted the Germans and
Spaniards to accept a floating body as that of a victim of an aircraft disaster, and would neither ask
me why nor seek to find an answer elsewhere.

So I rang up Sir Bernard and we arranged a meeting at his club, the Junior Carlton. There, over a
glass of sherry, I put our problem to him. After a
moment or two of thought, he gave me one of those
concise, yet complete, expositions that had convinced so many juries—and even so many judges.
His advice gave me hope. If the body was floating
in a "Mae West" when it was recovered, we could
use one of a man who had either drowned or died
from any but a few of the "natural causes"; victims of an aircraft disaster at sea sometimes died
from an injury received in the crash, and some died
from drowning, but many died from exposure or
even from shock; our field of search was less nar-
row than I had feared it might be.

My opinion of Sir Bernard was fully justified; that
extraordinary man listened to my questions and
gave me his answers without ever for a moment giving vent to the curiosity which he must have felt.
He asked me some questions which bore on the
pathological problem that I was putting to him, but

never once did he ask why I wanted to know or what I was proposing to do.

But even then the quest was not easy. We could not make any open inquiries—at all costs we had to avoid anything which might start talk. We could not risk anyone remembering that someone had been trying to obtain a dead body, and such a search was just the sort of thing that is likely to start gossip: "Have you heard? It's frightfully odd. So-and-So was asking Such-and-Such the other day where he could get a dead body." And so, very quietly, our search went on. There we were, in 1942, surrounded all too often by dead bodies, but none that we could take. We felt like the Ancient Mariner—bodies, bodies, everywhere, nor any one to take! We felt like Pirandello—"Six officers in search of a corpse."

At one time we feared that we might have to do a body-snatch—"do a Burke and Hare" as one of us put it; but we did not like that idea, if we could possibly avoid it. We managed to make some very guarded inquiries from a few Service medical officers whom we could trust; but when we heard of a possibility, either the relatives were unlikely to agree or we could not trust those whose permission we would need not to mention to other close relatives what had happened—or there were some other snags, such as a complication in the cause of death.

At last, when we had begun to feel that it would

have either to be a "Burke and Hare" after all or
we would have to extend our inquiries so widely as
to risk suspicion of our motives turning into gossip,
we heard of someone who had just died from pneu-
monia after exposure: pathologically speaking, it
looked as if he might answer our requirements. We
made feverish inquiries into his past and about his
relatives; we were soon satisfied that these would not
talk or pass on such information as we could give
them. But there was still the crucial question: could
we get permission to use the body without saying
what we proposed to do with it and why? All we
could possibly tell anyone was that we could guarantee that the purpose would be a really worthwhile
one, as anything that was done would be with approval on the highest level, and that the remains
would eventually receive proper burial, though
under a false name.

Permission, for which our indebtedness is great,
was obtained on condition that I should never let it
be known whose corpse it was. It must therefore
suffice for me to say that the body was that of a
young man in his early thirties. He had not been
very physically fit for some time before his death,
but we could accept that for, as I said to a senior
officer who queried the point, "He does not have to
look like an officer—only like a staff officer."

As a precaution, I had another chat with Sir Bernard Spilsbury. He was quite satisfied: the pneu-

monia was a help, for there would tend to be some liquid in the lungs, as might well be the case if the man had died while floating in a rough sea. If a post mortem examination was made by someone who had formed the preconceived idea that the death was probably due to drowning there was little likelihood that the difference between this liquid, in lungs that had started to decompose, and sea water would be noticed. Sir Bernard closed our talk with the characteristically confident statement: "You have nothing to fear from a Spanish post mortem; to detect that this young man had not died after an aircraft had been lost at sea would need a pathologist of my experience—and there aren't any in Spain."

So we arranged for the body to be kept in suitable cold storage until we were ready for it.

3.

"OPERATION MINCEMEAT"

I NOW HAD TO GET general approval for the principle of the operation. The first step, as always before any operation, was to get a code name; except in the case of a few major operations for which the Prime Minister himself invented the names, these were always taken from lists issued by us to the Service departments and the various Commands. I therefore went to see what names had been allocated for Admiralty use, and there I found that the word "Mincemeat" had just been restored after employment in a successful operation some time before. My sense of humor having by this time become somewhat macabre, the word seemed to be one of good omen—and "Operation Mincemeat" it became.

17

I had next to decide where we were to send the
body, and I chose Huelva as the best destination, if
delivery there was possible. For we knew that there
was a very active German agent at Huelva who had
excellent contacts with certain Spaniards, both officials and others. If the body reached Huelva, the
odds were very heavy that this agent would be given
any papers or other objects of importance that might
be with it; even if circumstances prevented that hap-
pening, there was no doubt whatsoever that he would
either get copies or be given detailed information,
and we could then be sure that he would alert his
superiors in Madrid who would intercept the documents at a higher level. Our only risk was that the
body and papers would be handed straight over to
the British Vice-Consul so quickly that no one could
intercept anything. But the co-operation between the
Spaniards and the Germans was so complete that
such a proper procedure was most improbable: if
there were a Spaniard who proposed to do that, I
had little doubt but that there would be several
others who would step in and prevent it.

Huelva had a further advantage in that it was not
too near to Gibraltar; we did not want the Spaniards
to send the body for burial there. The arrival at Gibraltar of the body of an officer who did not really
exist might give rise to talk which would be almost
certain to be picked up by the many German agents

who obtained information through the Spaniards who entered and left that area each day.

So I went to the Hydrographer of the Navy at the Admiralty and made some inquiries about weather and tidal conditions at various points off the coast of Spain at various times of the year. Our luck was holding. Although the tidal stream would not be too helpful and would set along the coast, the south-westerly wind, which would be the prevailing wind in April, would be "onshore." Indeed, the Hydrographer thought that "an object" would probably drift in towards the shore, and a body in a "Mae West" would be comparatively more affected by the wind than would the sort of object which I had led him to envisage.

So Huelva was decided on. There was practically no doubt that the body would float inshore: then, if the normal procedure was followed, the body would be handed over to the British Vice-Consul for burial. And, as I have said, we were confident that the efficiency of the local German agent would ensure that any papers, or at least copies of them, would eventually reach the Germans. Our confidence in him was not misplaced.

While we were going into the exact location for "Mincemeat's" arrival, a means of transportation had to be devised. He could not be dropped for fear of injury, which left three methods of placing him in the sea: submarine, flying boat or a temporary diversion of one of the ships which escorted the convoys up the coast of Spain. Of these a submarine could clearly get much the closest inshore without risk of detection. I therefore asked permission from the Vice-Chief of Naval Staff (Lord Home) to discuss possibilities with Admiral Barry, the Flag Officer commanding our submarines: it was, of course, on the basis that our planning was purely tentative, so that a complete scheme could be worked out for submission to the Chiefs of Staff.

Admiral Barry readily saw the possibilities of the idea, and I had a preliminary talk with his Chief Staff Officer. He decided that "Mincemeat" could be carried in a submarine on passage to Malta, as these quite frequently took important but not too bulky articles to that island. We discussed whether the body should be transported in the casing (that is under what would normally be called the deck) or inside the actual pressure hull of the submarine. In spite of the size of the container, which would have to be some six feet, six inches long, and about two feet in diameter, he considered that it could be accommodated inside the pressure hull and brought up through the conning tower for launching at sea. This greatly eased our problem, as it meant that we would only have to get an airtight canister and not a pressure-proof container, which would have had to be much heavier and more complicated. The question remained whether the body could be kept in a plain canister for the necessary time, after removal from cold storage, without decomposition being too great —or would we have to try to get some form of enormous thermos flask?

So I consulted Sir Bernard Spilsbury once more. He took the view that temperature would be of comparatively minor importance if the body was really cold when it was put into the container. The important thing was to exclude as much oxygen as possible, as it was that which hastened decomposition. He advised that the best method for us to use would be to stand our container on one end and fill it with dry ice; as that melted into carbon dioxide, it would prevent air from entering. We should then lower the body carefully into the canister and pack it round once more with dry ice. If that was done carefully, there should be little oxygen left in the container, and the rate of decomposition would be so slowed down that, if the body was picked up shortly after launching, its condition would be consistent with a few days' immersion floating in from an aircraft crash some distance offshore.

So we arranged for a container to be made of two skins of 22-gauge sheet steel welded together, with asbestos wool between the skins; at the top there was a similar lid which was bedded on to an airtight rubber gasket by sixteen nuts; a box-spanner was chained to the lid, to which it was clipped when not in use; a lifting handle was provided at each

end, for it would weigh over 400 pounds with the
body inside.

To complete the account of this part of our preparations, I should record that later on I saw Admiral
Barry again and told him that the plan was going
ahead and that, if we got final approval, we would
want the operation carried out at about the end of
April. This would also have the advantage from the
submarine's point of view of there being little or no
moon, so as to render detection close inshore less
likely. He decided that H.M. Submarine *Seraph*
might be used, as she could delay her departure for
Malta by a fortnight, spending the time "working
up" in home waters. The chance of using *Seraph*
was fortunate, as she was commanded by Lieutenant
Jewell, and he and his ship's company had already
had experience of special operations in connection
with the North Africa landings. They had picked up
General Giraud on his escape from captivity and it
was they who had put General Mark Clark ashore
on the coast of North Africa when he made secret
contact with the French, and then taken him off
again.

I had prepared tentative "operation orders" for
the Captain of the submarine, and these Admiral
Barry approved; but, at his suggestion, Lieutenant
Jewell came to the Flag Officer, Submarines Headquarters, where he and I could talk over the whole
matter.

I gave him the "operation orders," which were as follows:

OPERATION MINCEMEAT

1. *Object*

To cause a briefcase containing documents to drift ashore as near as possible to HUELVA in Spain in such circumstances that it will be thought to have been washed ashore from an aircraft which crashed at sea when the case was being taken by an officer from the U.K. to Allied Forces H.Q. in North Africa.

2. *Method*

A dead body dressed in the battledress uniform of a Major, Royal Marines, and wearing a "Mae West," will be taken out in a submarine, together with the briefcase and a rubber dinghy.

The body will be packed fully clothed and ready (and wrapped in a blanket to prevent friction) in a tubular airtight container (which will be labeled as "Optical Instruments").

The container is just under 6 feet 6 inches long and just under 2 feet in diameter and has no excrescences of any kind on the sides. The end which opens has a flush-fitting lid which is held tightly in position by a number of nuts and has fitted on its exterior in clips a box-spanner with a permanent tommy-bar which is chained to the lid.

Both ends are fitted with handles which fold down flat. It will be possible to lift the container by using both handles or even by using the handle in the lid alone, but it would be better not to take the whole weight on the handle at the other end, as the steel of which the container is made is of light gauge to keep the weight as low as possible. The approximate total weight when the container is full will be 400 pounds.

When the container is closed the body will be packed round with a certain amount of dry ice. The container should therefore be opened on deck, as the dry ice will give off carbon dioxide.

3. *Position*

The body should be put into the water as close inshore as prudently possible and as near to HUELVA as possible, preferably to the northwest of the river mouth.

According to the Hydrographic Department, the tides in that area run mainly up and down the coast, and every effort should therefore be made to choose a period with an onshore wind. Southwesterly winds are in fact the prevailing winds in that area at this time of year.

The latest information about the tidal streams in that area, as obtained from the Superintendent of Tides, is attached.

4. *Delivery of the Package*

The package will be brought up to the port of departure by road on whatever day is desired, preferably as close to the sailing day as possible. The briefcase will be handed over at the same time to the Captain of the submarine. The rubber dinghy will also be a separate parcel.

5. *Disposal of the Body*

When the body is removed from the container all that will be necessary will be to fasten the chain attached to the briefcase through the belt of the trench-coat, which will be the outer garment on the body. The chain is of the type worn under the coat, round the chest and out through the sleeve. At the end is a "dog-lead" type of clip for attaching to the handle of the briefcase and a similar clip for forming the loop round the chest. It is this loop that should be made through the belt of the trench-coat as if the officer has slipped the chain off for comfort in the aircraft, but has nevertheless kept it attached to him so that the bag should not either be forgotten or slide away from him in the aircraft.

The body should then be deposited in the water, as should also be the rubber dinghy. As this should drift at a different speed from the body, the exact position at which it is released is unimportant, but it should be near the body, but not too near if that is possible.

6. *Those in the Know at Gibraltar*

Steps have been taken to inform F.O.I.C.[1] Gibraltar and his S.O.(I).[2] No one else there will be in the picture.

7. *Signals*

If the operation is successfully carried out, a signal

[1] Flag Officer in Charge. [2] Staff Officer, Intelligence.

should be made "MINCEMEAT completed." If that is made from Gibraltar the S.O.(I) should be asked to send it addressed to D.N.I.[3] (PERSONAL). If it can be made earlier it should be made in accordance with orders from F.O.S.[4]

8. *Cancellation*

If the operation has to be cancelled a signal will be made "Cancel MINCEMEAT." In that case the body and container should be sunk in deep water; as the container may have positive buoyancy, it may either have to be weighted or water may have to be allowed to enter. In the latter case care must be taken that the body does not escape. The briefcase should be handed to the S.O.(I) at Gibraltar, with instructions to burn the contents unopened, if there is no possibility of taking that course earlier. The rubber dinghy should be handed to the S.O. (I) for disposal.

9. *Abandonment*

If the operation has to be abandoned, a signal should be made "MINCEMEAT abandoned" as soon as possible (see Para. 7 above).

10. *Cover*

This is a matter for consideration. Until the operation actually takes place, it is thought that the labelling of

---

[3] Director of Naval Intelligence. [4] Flag Officer, Submarines (Admiral Barry).

the container "Optical Instruments" will provide sufficient cover. It is suggested that the cover after the operation has been completed should be that it is hoped to trap a very active German agent in this neighborhood, and it is hoped that sufficient evidence can be obtained by this means to get the Spaniards to eject him. The importance of dealing with this man should be impressed on the crew, together with the fact that any leakage that may *ever* take place about this will compromise our power to get the Spaniards to act in such cases; also that they will never learn whether we were successful in this objective, as the whole matter will have to be conducted in secrecy with the Spaniards or we won't be able to get them to act.

It is in fact most important that the Germans and Spaniards should accept these papers in accordance with Para. 1. If they should suspect that the papers are a "plant," it might have far-reaching consequences of great magnitude.

(*Signed*) E. E. S. MONTAGU,
Lt.-Cdr., R.N.V.R.
31.3.43.

We then discussed the operation and filled in points of detail.

While all these things were being arranged, we had been busy over the more interesting matters. What document could we provide which could be so impressive that it would make the Germans alter their planning and disposition of forces? How could we provide the document with a sufficiently convincing background to make them accept it as genuine; for Pooh-Bah was right when he spoke of " . . . corroborative detail, intended to give artistic verisimilitude to an otherwise bald and unconvincing narrative."

4

THE
VITAL
DOCUMENT

ONE THING seemed to me to be crystal clear: if purpose of this document was to deceive the Germans *so that they would act upon it,* then it had to be on a really high level; no indiscretion or "leak" from an officer of normal rank would do. Even a security lapse from one brigadier, air commodore or rear-admiral to another would not be weighty enough.

If the German General Staff was to be persuaded, in face of all probabilities, to bank on our next target being somewhere other than Sicily, it would have to have before it a document which was passing between officers who *must* know what our real plans were, who could not possibly be mistaken and who could not themselves be the victims of a cover

plan. If the operation was to be worthwhile, I had
to have a document written by someone, and to
someone, whom the Germans knew—and whom they
knew to be "right in the know."

So I put up the proposal that General Sir Archibald Nye, the Vice-Chief of the Imperial General
Staff, should write the letter—and that he should
write it to General Alexander (who commanded an
army in Tunisia, under General Eisenhower) at
18th Army Group Headquarters. The letter should be
of what we junior officers called "the old boy type";
it should be on the lines of "Look here, old chap,
I want you to understand that we realize your problems, but we have our difficulties too. The C.I.G.S.[1]
has had to turn down some of your requests, although you're pressing for them. There really are
reasons why you can't have what you want just now,
and here they are. . . ." and so on: the sort of
friendly letter which can give information and ex-
planations that can't be put into an official com-
munication. That sort of letter, and that sort of letter only, could convey convincingly to the Germans
the indication that our next target was not Sicily,
and yet could be found in the possession of an officer and not in a bag full of the usual official
documents going from home to our army abroad.

I was aiming high—and I had to. I expected

[1] Chief of the Imperial General Staff.

something of an explosion—and I got it! For many of even the most able and efficient people failed to appreciate what was wanted for this sort of job; for to realize that needed a particular sort of approach and a peculiar sort of mind that could look at the same puzzle from several different angles at the same time.

You are a British Intelligence officer; you have an opposite number in the enemy Intelligence, say (as in the last war), in Berlin; and above him is the German Operational Command. What you, a Briton with a British background, think can be deduced from a document does not matter. It is what *your opposite number,* with his German knowledge and background, will think that matters—what construction *he* will put on the document. Therefore, if you want *him* to think such-and-such a thing, you must give him something which will make *him* (and not *you*) think it. But he may be suspicious and want confirmation; you must think out what inquiries will *he* make (not what inquiries would *you* make) and give him the answers to those inquiries so as to satisfy him. In other words, you must remember that a German does not think and react as an Englishman does, and you must put yourself into his mind.

But you must not forget the Operational Staff to whom he reports and whom he has to convince if you are to succeed in your plot. The German Operational Staff does not know all the Allied difficulties—for example, how short you are of, say, land-ing-craft—and they may be prepared to believe that an operation is possible which your own Opera-tional Staff know is not on the cards at all; you have to remember that your plan has to deceive *them*, and not your own Staff. But it is not everyone who can remember, *and apply*, those considerations.

And so we ran into difficulties. But before I re-cord them I should say a word or two about "cover targets" and "cover plans." If you are to prevent there being a concentration at your target ready to meet your landing you must try to draw the enemy's defensive effort and forces elsewhere; if possible, he should be convinced that you won't attack your real target, but will attack somewhere else—that you will attack what we called the "cover target." As I have already mentioned, it is usually certain that there will be some leakage that an operation is intended, and the security measures designed to prevent such leakage giving away the real target may sometimes be adapted to fulfil a second purpose also—to help to put over the cover target. For instance, if any leakage did occur about the operation which I have instanced against the Lofoten Islands, and if sun helmets had been issued, the leakage might well be such that the enemy would deduce that the target was somewhere tropical. If the ships which were to transport the troops received charts or other infor-mation which indicated the chosen cover target (let us say Dakar), the various leakages which reached the Germans from those and other factors might well be added together by the German Intelligence Service to make the picture that you wanted them to have.

The best possible cover target would be one so far away from the real one that any sea, air or land defenses that the enemy might prepare would be well clear of the real target. To give an exaggerated example: if you were going to invade North Africa and could persuade the enemy that you were going into Norway (oh, what a happy dream!), any extra defenses that he put into Norway could not possibly interfere with your real operation.

But in actual war the cover target may have to be in the same general area as the real target, and then it is impossible to divert the whole of the enemy's defenses. For instance, if at the time of our North Africa landings in 1942 we had put over a cover target of a landing in Rommel's rear at, say, Tobruk—and if we had succeeded in convincing the Germans—we might have succeeded in diverting some military forces and perhaps the Luftwaffe to that area, but the U-boats would have been drawn to the Straits of Gibraltar through which the real convoys would have to pass for the genuine operation. Often, therefore, it is the case of a compromise between what would be a perfect cover target and what it is possible to get the enemy to believe.

When we came to relate this theory to the particular problem which faced our Intelligence team, our task was to try to convince the Germans that we were not going to attack Sicily—the target which must have been obvious to them—and to persuade them to move their forces elsewhere and to use up time and effort in strengthening the defenses of other places.

Looking at the situation from the Allied angle, we had an army under General Eisenhower based on French North Africa at the western end of the Mediterranean and another army under Field-Marshal Sir Henry Wilson based on Egypt, together holding the whole North Africa coast. We knew that it was intended that both these great forces should be used for a single operation. There were many reasons for this decision which it would take too long to detail here, but I can summarize them in brief by saying that an assault on the defended coast of Sicily, followed by an advance up the peninsula of Italy, would need all the forces that we had available. Apart from the actual troops and aircraft engaged, there was a considerable shortage of landing-craft and the task of providing the shipping and escorts necessary to supply and maintain the campaign would preclude the conduct of two campaigns at once.

When we looked at the same problem from the German viewpoint, the picture was somewhat different. So far as they knew, the Allies could use General Eisenhower's army in the western Mediterranean to attack the South of France, although this would probably necessitate the reduction of Sicily, Sardinia and Corsica, and would be a risky operation with Italy as an unconquered base for counter-attacks on the flank of our supply lines. Equally, the same army or the army based on Egypt could be used for an attack on Italy, although, if the western army was to be used for this purpose, it would almost certainly necessitate the conquest of Sicily as a first step. Finally the eastern army could be used for an invasion of Greece and an advance through the Balkans.

There was no reason to believe that the Germans knew of our shortage of landing-craft, and it was quite possible that they could be led to believe that we were going to mount two operations, one in the western Mediterranean with General Eisenhower's army and one in the eastern Mediterranean with Sir Henry Wilson's army.

When our team considered the deception that we wanted to convey by "Operation Mincemeat," we reasoned as follows: as the Allies had most of their forces in Tunisia, it was hopeless to try to persuade the Germans that we would take our convoys from there through the narrows past their airfields in Sicily. Therefore, any cover target would have to be somewhere west of Italy if the Germans were to be-

lieve that it represented the operation in which
these troops were involved. Sardinia had already
been chosen as the official cover target so as to pre-
tend that we were going to by-pass Sicily and take
Sardinia and Corsica, thus opening the whole of
the coast of Italy and southern France to attack.

But it seemed to me that, as we would not have
to rely on a series of leaks which might or might
not reach the Germans, but could use a single document, there could be a second string to our bow. I
felt that we could probably convince the Germans
that Sir Henry Wilson's army under General Montgomery was not going to take part in the same operation as General Eisenhower's, and that it was
going to conduct an invasion of Greece and an advance up the Balkans. There did not seem to be any
reason why they should not be led to believe in a
double operation with an assault at each end of the
Mediterranean, and if we could succeed in convincing them of this we could get a much wider dis-
persal of their forces than if we based our deception
only on the "official" cover target of Sardinia.

I therefore proposed that the letter to General
Alexander should reveal that there were to be two
operations: his, under General Eisenhower's command, against Sardinia and perhaps Corsica, with
another under Field-Marshal Sir Henry Wilson
against Greece. I suggested also that the letter
should reveal that we were going to *try to convince*

the Germans that we were going to invade Sicily!
It seemed to me that the beauty of this was that if
there were any actual leakage of our real plans, the
Germans would think that what was in fact a leakage was only part of the cover that they had read
about in the letter. If they swallowed our deception
—that one letter—they would disbelieve any genuine
information that might leak through.

So the proposal was put up to the Chiefs of Staff
—and then the trouble started! Not many people
saw the proposal, for the "usual channels" were by-
passed; but even then, as the plan and the rough
draft of the document went up and down to the
Chiefs of Staff and back again, everyone who felt
himself to be an expert, and to know the German
mind, had bright ideas. It was too dangerous, they
said, to try for high stakes, and the letter should be
a low-level one, merely putting over a false date;
we would never get the Germans to swallow the
story and we would be bound to pinpoint Sicily; we
must not mention Sardinia as the supposed real target, as, if the Germans saw through the deception,
that would pinpoint Sicily.

Perhaps the greatest achievement of the whole operation was to persuade our masters that this was
an opportunity that would never recur, and that if
we were to achieve a real success we must aim high.
I have little doubt, as I look back, that to deceive

the German High Command was nothing like as difficult as it was to persuade their British opposite numbers that we could do that.

Fortunately, after a while, Sir Archibald Nye himself got really intrigued; he tried a letter, based on my draft, which he suggested might do. It had to be pointed out that, although it indicated the cover targets in just the right sort of way, it would be wholly unconvincing; it was the sort of straightforward letter which could and would go in an official bag and would never be given to an officer to carry in his pocket. This was a challenge to which Sir Archibald rose wonderfully, and he produced a truly magnificent letter. To help the deception, in case the Germans heard of "Husky" (the real code name for the invasion of Sicily), he used that as the code name for the eastern operation against Greece, and used "Brimstone," a fake code name, for the western operation against Sardinia. His draft ran as follows:

Telephone: Whitehall 9400.
Chief of the Imperial
    General Staff.

War Office,
Whitehall,
London, S.W.1.
23rd April, 1943.

Personal and Most Secret

MY DEAR ALEX,

I am taking advantage of sending you a personal letter by hand of one of Mountbatten's officers, to give you the inside history of our recent exchange of cables about Mediterranean operations and their attendant cover plans. You may have felt our decisions were somewhat arbitrary, but I can assure you in fact that the C.O.S. Committee [1] gave the most careful consideration both to your recommendation and also to Jumbo's. [2]

We have had recent information that the Boche have been reinforcing and strengthening their defences in Greece and Crete and C.I.G.S. felt that our forces for the assault were insufficient. It was agreed by the Chiefs of Staff that the 5th Division should be reinforced by one Brigade Group for the assault on the beach south of CAPE ARAXOS and that a similar reinforcement should be made for the 56th Division at KALAMATA. We are earmarking the necessary forces and shipping.

Jumbo Wilson had proposed to select SICILY as cover target for "HUSKY"; but we have already chosen it as cover for operation "BRIMSTONE." The C.O.S. Committee went into the whole question exhaustively again and came to the conclusion that in view of the preparations in Algeria, the amphibious training which will be taking place on the Tunisian coast and the heavy air bombardment which will be put down to neutralise the Sicilian airfields, we should stick to our plan of making it cover for "BRIMSTONE"—indeed, we stand a very good chance of making him think we will go for Sicily—it is an obvious objective and one about which he must be nervous. On the other hand, they felt there wasn't much hope of per-

---

[1] Chiefs of Staff Committee. [2] Nickname of Field-Marshal Sir Henry Wilson, Commander-in-Chief, Middle East.

suading the Boche that the extensive preparations in the eastern Mediterranean were also directed at SICILY. For this reason they have told Wilson his cover plan should be something nearer the spot, e.g. the Dodecanese. Since our relations with Turkey are now so obviously closer the Italians must be pretty apprehensive about these islands.

I imagine you will agree with these arguments. I know you will have your hands more than full at the moment and you haven't much chance of discussing future operations with Eisenhower. But if by any chance you do want to support Wilson's proposal, I hope you will let us know soon, because we can't delay much longer.

I am very sorry we weren't able to meet your wishes about the new commander of the Guards Brigade. Your own nominee was down with a bad attack of 'flu and not likely to be really fit for another few weeks. No doubt, however, you know Forster personally; he has done extremely well in command of a brigade at home, and is, I think, the best fellow available.

You must be about as fed up as we are with the whole question of war medals and 'Purple Hearts.' We all agree with you that we don't want to offend our American friends, but there is a good deal more to it than that. If our troops who happen to be serving in one particular theatre are to get extra decorations merely because the Americans happen to be serving there too, we will be faced with a good deal of discontent among those troops fighting elsewhere perhaps just as bitterly— or more so. My own feeling is that we should thank the Americans for their kind offer, but say firmly it would cause too many anomalies and we are sorry we can't accept. But it is on the agenda for the next Military Members Meeting and I hope you will have a decision very soon.

> Best of luck.
>> Yours ever,
>>> ARCHIE NYE.

General the Hon. Sir Harold R. L.G. Alexander,
G.C.B., C.S.I., D.S.O., M.C.,
Headquarters,
18th Army Group.

Nothing could have been better; it carried out the scheme put up to him in a way that only someone who was himself fully in the picture of the personal relationships among high officers could have devised. Quite by inference, and so accidentally as to prevent the Germans thinking it a plant, it makes it clear that there will be an eastern Mediterranean operation with a landing in Greece, and it also makes it clear that we *want* the Germans to think that the western Mediterranean operation will be in Sicily (so *that* obviously *can't* be the real target); it does all that in an "off the record" atmosphere which, together with the very personal matters in the rest of the letter, makes it natural that it should not go through an official channel.

I had only two regrets. The first was that, knowing my Germans, I wanted to make certain that they had an absolutely definite target on which to fix as

our western objective; but the Chiefs of Staff re-
fused to sanction any mention of Sardinia in the letter; they thought that it would pinpoint Sicily too
clearly if the Germans saw through our operation.
However, after the Prime Minister's completely real-
istic appreciation of the situation, which I have already mentioned, I managed to get a joking reference to Sardinia inserted into another letter that
we eventually drafted for Lord Louis Mountbatten
to sign—and that, as will be seen, was of considerable
value.

My second regret was less serious. I had wanted
to include in the letter something which would appeal to the mind of the German reader as being consistent with thoughts that he already had. I felt that
the average mind is readier to believe in the accuracy of a document if some part of it contains
what he already knows. I had thought that the best
way of getting an innocuous reference of this kind
into the letter was to suggest a leg-pull of General
Montgomery which might well coincide with the
rather heavy-footed German humor. I therefore suggested that Sir Archibald should ask General Alexander, "What's gone wrong with Monty? He hasn't
issued an Order of the Day for at least a week."
Not long before this time General Montgomery had
been issuing a number of Orders of the Day to encourage the troops, and a certain amount of ribaldry
had resulted in various quarters. However, for some

reason that I have never wholly fathomed, the Chiefs of Staff firmly banned my joke. I admit that it was a poor one, and its loss was not important, although I felt sure that the Germans would study and appreciate any joke of that kind.

Sir Archibald's letter was typed on his notepaper, addressed "My Dear Alex" and signed by him, and then enclosed and sealed in the usual double envelopes. The vital document was ready, and it was a pleasing touch that it happened to bear the date of St. George's Day.

5.

MAJOR MARTIN, ROYAL MARINES

WHILE WE WERE PREPARING the document which
called the "vital letter" we had to consider the
"man" who was going to carry it, for it was obvious
that the first question that our opponent in Berlin
would ask was: "How did the letter come to be at
Huelva?" True, it was the sort of letter which would
be carried by an officer, and not in an official bag;
nevertheless, the German Intelligence officer would
ask: "*Was* it carried by an officer? Did he seem to
be a genuine officer?"

So we had to establish, as a first step, that the
body was that of an officer. He had no uniform that
we could use, as, for reasons both of security and
of keeping my promise to conceal his identity, it was

essential that we should provide him with a fresh uniform.

We had taken it for granted that, in his new personality, the body should be that of an army officer; this had, I think, followed in our minds from the fact that he was carrying a letter from the V.C.I.G.S. to the Commander-in-Chief of an army, and probably also from the fact that the wartime army was so large.

After a while, however, we decided against putting him in the army. There were a number of reasons for the decision, but the main and compelling one was concerned with the "distribution" of the signals and reports which would pass between the appropriate Attaché in Madrid and London after the body came ashore in Spain. Normally telegrams and signals were received in the appropriate office of the Service department concerned, and were then automatically distributed to such officers and departments as might be interested in the subject to which they referred, the distribution being based on a series of distribution lists. As a result, any telegram which reported the finding of a dead body on the Spanish beach would be sent to the Service department concerned and would be automatically distributed to quite a number of people, and any follow-up telegrams would receive the same distribution. Under the Admiralty system, it would be possible for me to arrange, with the authority of D.N.I., that this automatic distribution should be by-passed so that the messages resulting from our operation would be distributed to me only—and such an arrangement would not arouse comment. Under the War Office system, it was not easy to make any such arrangement for distribution to be limited either to me or to any colleague in the War Office.

So we decided that the body should not "join" the army, but would have to come under the Admiralty—and at once we found ourselves faced with a number of problems that we had not visualized. He could not easily become a naval officer because, while an army officer could make such a flight as we were envisaging from London to North African Headquarters wearing a battledress, a naval officer would have had to wear proper uniform—and although a battledress need not fit too accurately, naval uniform would have to be made to measure. We formed a horrid mental picture of Gieves' cutter being brought down to measure and fit our corpse for its uniform, and discarded that suggestion!

The only other possibility which would keep this "officer" under naval control was that he should join the Royal Marines: that would ease the problem of uniform, but it would bring a number of other problems. First, we had banked on the fact that the wartime army was so big that there were many units whose officers would not be astonished if they heard of an officer of their unit whom they did not know

existed, whereas the Royals are a small corps, and
even in wartime most of the officers know one
another—or at least know of one another. Second,
there was the difficulty of obtaining a photograph.
For various reasons, we had not got, and could not
get, any photograph of the young man whose body
we were using which was suitable for an identity
card in his new personality, and we had banked on
the fact that army officers did not carry identity cards
with photographs when going abroad—but Royal
Marine officers did.

We discussed these problems at some length; we
easily appreciated the danger that might be caused
by the small number that there was of Royal Marine
officers, and that if the body *was* sent by the Spaniards to Gibraltar for burial the danger that we had
anticipated if the body of an army officer was sent
there would be enormously increased; nevertheless,
we decided that, in view of the distance between
Huelva and Gibraltar, we could accept even the increased risk due to his being a Royal Marine. We decided also that we could accept the difficulty of providing a suitable photograph, but in this case we had
not appreciated how great the difficulty was.

First, we tried the expedient of taking photographs,
of the appropriate type, of the corpse; that was a
complete failure. It is a common criticism of photographs taken of living people for the subject to say,
"Oh, it makes me look as if I were dead!" Such criti-

cism may or may not be justified, but I defy anyone
to take a photograph of someone who *is* dead and to
make it look as if he could conceivably be alive: it
is impossible to describe how utterly and hopelessly
dead any photograph of the body looked.

So a feverish search took place for a "double" of
the corpse—or even someone who resembled him sufficiently for a poor photo to give a reasonable appearance of what the owner of the body must have
looked like in life. It was an odd thing, but although
we had not thought that our young man had had an
appearance which would have singled him out in a
crowd, we could not find the man we wanted. All
of us walked about for days staring rudely at anyone with whom we came in contact and who might,
on some excuse, be persuaded to sit for his photo;
eventually I decided to ask a young naval officer
working in N.I.D.[1] to put on a battledress blouse
and let us photograph him—I forget what excuse I
used. The result, as I had anticipated, was not too
good, but we decided that the likeness would suffice,
bearing in mind the poor quality of such photographs.

And then we had another stroke of luck. Sitting
opposite to me at a meeting to deal with quite a
different matter, I saw someone who might have been
the twin brother of the corpse; he was readily per-

[1] Naval Intelligence Division.

suaded to let us photograph him, and that obstacle was surmounted.

The final step, before we could "commission" the body as an officer, was to give him a name and a rank. I felt that a very junior officer would be unlikely to be given such a letter as the vital document to carry, but we could not make him too senior for several reasons; the most important was that our body was too young to have achieved very high rank unless he had been so outstandingly able that his brother officers would be bound to have heard of him. I therefore decided that I would make him a captain (acting major); then I sat down with a *Navy List;* I steadily went through the list of Royal Marine officers until I found a little group of about that same rank who all had the same name: that name was "Martin."

There seemed to me to be an advantage in a group of that kind. If the death of a "Major Martin" *did* arouse discussion in a wardroom, there was always a hope that those present would not know all the Martins in the Royal Marines—or that, if they did, they would think that there was an error in the initial given and would not know whether to write and "condole." It might not have worked out that way (indeed for all I knew all the Martins were brothers), but this was only an added precaution against a not too serious risk—and, of course, there was bound to be some risk in any name that I gave him. So I added

the good normal Christian name of "William," and
our body became "Captain (Acting Major) William
Martin, Royal Marines," with the approval of the
Commandant-General, Royal Marines, who agreed to
accept him into that corps. Finally, I laid on the necessary precautions in case any inquiries were addressed to the C.G.R.M.'s department.

I had got a blank identity card and spent my time,
whenever seated, rubbing it up and down my trouser
leg to try to produce the "patina" which such a document normally gets with time, even when carried in
a wallet. I did not do so badly, but I was a little
worried by the slow progress of the aging process
when I got another idea. I decided that Major Martin should have lost his original identity card and
have had a new one issued. So I got a new blank,
stuck in the photograph of Major Martin's double,
filled in the particulars and signed it for him, and
then got a suitable official to sign it as issued on the
2nd February 1943, "in lieu of No. 09650 lost"—the
latter number being that of my own card, which
would help to reduce complications if there were
any subsequent inquiry—and got the appropriate
stamps and seals put on it.

I had decided that Major Martin's "ship" should be
Combined Operations H.Q., for reasons that I will
deal with shortly, and chose Cardiff as his birthplace
for no particular reason. The card being complete, I

then proceeded to give it a reasonable degree of aging by the trouser-rubbing process.

So the basis of Major Martin's personality was established; anyone finding his body could find *who* he was from his identity card. But I was sure that my German friends in Huelva, Madrid, or Berlin would want to know *why* Major Martin was going to North Africa: if we could let them find evidence answering that question it would increase faith in the "vital letter."

Why *should* a Royal Marine officer be flown out to North Africa? And why should he be flown out in such circumstances that the Vice-Chief of the Imperial General Staff would know of his going so that he could be entrusted with an important letter? Why?

After some thought, I found a reason which seemed plausible to our team. A seaborne operation was being mounted against a defended coast; this would involve the use of landing-craft, and it might well be that some hitch in training would call for assistance from an expert in that line; Major Martin could be that expert, and we decided to give him a document that made that clear.

I therefore drafted a letter for signature by Lord Louis Mountbatten, the Chief of Combined Operations, addressed to Admiral Sir Andrew Cunningham, Commander-in-Chief, Mediterranean. It was as follows:

In reply quote: S.R. 1924/43
Combined Operations Headquarters,
1A Richmond Terrace,
Whitehall, S.W.1.
21st April, 1943.

DEAR ADMIRAL OF THE FLEET,

I promised V.C.I.G.S. that Major Martin would arrange with you for the onward transmission of a letter he has with him for General Alexander. It is very urgent and very "hot" and as there are some remarks in it that could not be seen by others in the War Office, it could not go by signal. I feel sure that you will see that it goes on safely and without delay.

I think you will find Martin the man you want. He is quiet and shy at first, but he really knows his stuff. He was more accurate than some of us about the probable run of events at Dieppe and he has been well in on the experiments with the latest barges and equipment which took place up in Scotland.

Let me have him back, please, as soon as the assault is over. He might bring some sardines with him—they are "on points" here!

Yours sincerely,
LOUIS MOUNTBATTEN.

Admiral of the Fleet Sir A. B. Cunningham,
G.C.B., D.S.O.,
Commander in Chief Mediterranean,
Allied Forces H.Q.,
Algiers.

I was rather pleased with that letter. It explained

why Major Martin had the "vital letter" and why that had not been sent through official channels. It explained why Major Martin was being flown out. And, in view of the Prime Minister's clear realization that it would not matter if Sicily was pinpointed by a failure of our operation, I was enabled to make a reference to Sardinia; I did this by a joke which was frightfully labored, but I thought that that sort of joke would appeal to the Germans, who would be able to see the point and understand the reference. This joke, with its indication of Sardinia, was destined to play a part in our eventual success.

But there was yet one more ruse concealed in it. I was sure that the Germans in Berlin would get the "vital letter" or at least a copy of it, but I could not be sure that they would get more than a précis of what might be called the supporting documents, and I wanted to make certain that they would get this letter in full. I wanted Berlin to have the joke about Sardinia and I wanted them to have the explanation of why this officer was flying out and was carrying the unusual "vital document"; so I put in the bit about Dieppe. I was sure that no German could resist passing on to his superiors what he would feel to be an admission by the Chief of Combined Operations that our raid on Dieppe was not the success that we had hoped it would be. Whether or not I had accurately penetrated the German mind, this was the only one of Major Martin's documents, in addition to the vital document, of which we found a complete copy in the German files and which we know was studied in full by the German Intelligence in Berlin.

The letter was duly typed at Combined Operations H.Q., signed by Lord Louis, and given a fictitious, but plausible, reference number.

In the end we gave Major Martin one more letter to carry in addition to his personal papers. We were a little worried by the fact that an officer would probaby put two normal-sized envelopes into his pocket, or perhaps into his personal kit in spite of the secrecy of one of them. If Major Martin were to do this we had no absolute guarantee that the Spaniards would find them before handing over the body. We did not want to risk the German agent at Huelva having to curse his Spanish minions for not having searched the body. If only Major Martin could have an excuse for carrying the letters in a briefcase! We had to find him one.

It so happened that the official "pamphlet" on the Commandos by Hilary Saunders was about to be published in this country, and was to be accompanied by an American edition. We decided that it would be plausible for Lord Louis Mountbatten to have written a letter to General Eisenhower asking him for a Foreword for inclusion in the pamphlet. So a letter was drafted, making the request, and enclosing the proofs of that pamphlet and the photographs

which it would contain, and we took the opportunity
to include another little indication that Major Martin
was a very responsible officer. This letter ran as follows:

> In reply quote: S.R. 1989/43.
> Combined Operations Headquarters,
> 1A Richmond Terrace,
> Whitehall, S.W.1.
> 22nd April, 1943.

DEAR GENERAL,

I am sending you herewith two copies of the pamphlet
which has been prepared describing the activities of my
Command; I have also enclosed copies of the photographs which are to be included in the pamphlet.

The book has been written by Hilary St. George
Saunders, the English author of *Battle of Britain, Bomb-
er Command* and other pamphlets which have had a
great success both in this country and yours.

The edition which is to be published in the States has
already enjoyed pre-publication sales of nearly a million
and a half and I understand the American authorities will
distribute the book widely throughout the U. S. Army.

I understand from the British Information Service in
Washington that they would like a "message" from you
for use in the advertising for the pamphlet, and that they
have asked you direct, through Washington, for such a
message.

I am sending the proofs by hand of my Staff Officer,
Major W. Martin of the Royal Marines. I need not say
how honored we shall all be if you will give such a

message. I fully realize what a lot is being asked of you at a time when you are so fully occupied with infinitely more important matters. But I hope you may find a few minutes' time to provide the pamphlet with an expression of your invaluable approval so that it will be read widely and given every chance to bring its message of co-operation to our two peoples.

We are watching your splendid progress with admiration and pleasure and all wish we could be with you.

You may speak freely to Major Martin in this as well as any other matters since he has my entire confidence.

Yours sincerely,
LOUIS MOUNTBATTEN.

General Dwight Eisenhower,
Allied Forces H.Q., Algiers.

This letter also was signed by Lord Louis and, when put into an envelope with its enclosures, it fully justified Major Martin in using a briefcase in which to carry all his official documents.

But our problem over this point did not end here. We had found an excuse for presenting the official documents to the Spaniards in a way that allowed for any inefficiency on their part and made sure that the documents would be discovered, but had we been too clever? Just as we were congratulating ourselves on our ingenuity, a sudden qualm arose: how on earth were we to ensure that the body and the briefcase arrived in Huelva together? Although it might be possible to place the handle of the briefcase into

Major Martin's hand, we could not take the risk, on this all-important point, that the fingers might open and let the briefcase be dragged away by the sea. I made inquiries about *rigor mortis*, but, when I had added the complication that the body would have been frozen and then allowed to thaw, it was clear that the imponderables were far too many.

The only solution which we could devise was one which did not appeal to us, because it was the only point in the whole "set-up" which did not ring true. We decided to assume that an officer who carried really secret and important papers might attach his briefcase to one of the leather covered chains which some bank-messengers use—wearing them down their sleeves so they are not visible to the normal glance, but prevent their bag of valuables being snatched out of their hands. Such an arrangement seemed horribly phoney to us, but then *we* knew that this method was not one used by British officers. We decided that we would have to take a chance and rely on our opposite numbers in Berlin swallowing this feature. After all, *they* could not be sure that in no circumstances would a British officer adopt this method of safeguarding such documents.

So we decided to take the risk and use a chain. As may have been noted from the instructions to Lieutenant Jewell, we decided that Major Martin would not sit throughout a long flight with the briefcase dangling from his arm, and that it would be reasonable for him, instead of leaving this important bag to get lost or forgotten, to keep the bag on the chain, but to gain comfort by looping the latter through the belt of his trench coat.

It is hard to be dogmatic: maybe we worried too much; maybe, on the other hand, the Germans in Berlin would have become suspicious over this point, had it been reported to them. I will not anticipate at this stage what we learned later, and will therefore only say that our luck was good and that question was never put to the test. Still, I would dearly like to know whether the risk that we took was a justifiable one, for we took it on the basis that the Spaniards would report accurately on this obviously important point, but that our opponents would not be sufficiently sure that the chain was a flaw in an otherwise convincing picture for them to take the risk of rejecting the genuineness of the documents. We will never know whether we were right or not. Perhaps it is just as well that we won't!

Finally, as Major Martin was serving at Combined Operations H.Q., he needed a special pass, and we got him one. We felt that we were in danger of making Major Martin into too great a paragon of all the virtues, and that it was about time that he should show some human failing in addition to the loss of his identity card. As will be seen, we were also engaged on building up a personal character for him which would reveal him as a little careless in his personal affairs, in spite of his ability as an officer, and we could not divorce his personal characteristics completely from his military ones. Besides (as is recounted in the next chapter), an event had taken place in his life which would be likely to drive such trivialities as the renewal of a pass from his mind. We therefore decided that he should make the same slip as most of us had done at one time or another, and forget to renew his pass. The one that we gave him expired on the 31st March 1943; we were sure that it would not surprise the Germans (any more than it would us) if Major Martin had been able to get away with the use of this pass until his departure in the third or fourth week of April.

It only remained to provide Major Martin with his uniform. One of us who happened to have approximately the same build as Major Martin got a suitable battledress, to which we added Royal Marine and Commando flashes and a major's crown. An old trench coat was obtained, and we put similar badges of rank on the shoulder straps after having pierced them for the three "pips" of his substantive rank. Boots and webbing gaiters were got in addition to a shirt and all his underwear; these last were not new, but all old laundry-marks were removed from them and his handkerchiefs, and they were then all laundered together so as finally to have the same marks.

We had bought a shirt at Gieves, and we thought that Bill Martin might well have stuffed the scrumpled bill into the pocket of his trench coat. This produced the only real brick which we dropped: the officer who actually bought the shirt was not in the Navy, and he took the unbelievable step of paying cash. As Bill Martin hadn't an account there it would have been difficult for the officer to do otherwise without getting the wrong name on the bill, but, after the body was out of our reach, I suddenly realized that few naval officers had ever been known to pay cash to Gieves, least of all one who was being dunned for his overdraft! I could, however, comfort myself with the though that it was the *Germans* that we had to deceive; *they* could not know for certain whether temporary officers were still granted the same privileges by that long-suffering firm as were given to the Regulars. Still—it was a mistake and inartistic.

So the body of the "man who never was" had become that of an officer, Major Martin of the Royal Marines, and anyone who found the body would have ample evidence of who he was and why he was where he was. But it was still the body of an officer and not that of a person. We had still to provide him with his personal effects and with a human personality to make him "real."

6.

THE
CREATION
OF
A
PERSON

FROM QUITE AN EARLY STAGE Major Martin had become a real person to us and it was obviously desirable that as much of that feeling as possible should be shared by whoever investigated the body; the more real he appeared the more convincing the whole affair would be. Besides, I was quite sure that in a matter of this importance every little detail would be studied by the Germans in an effort to find a flaw in Major Martin's make-up, so as to be sure that the whole thing was genuine and not a plant. That I was not mistaken is evidenced by the fact that, as we learnt later, the Germans even noticed the dates on the two theatre-ticket stubs that we placed in Major Martin's pocket.

The method that we adopted in deciding on

Major Martin's personality was to keep on discussing him—rather as if we were pulling a friend to pieces behind his back. In fact, we talked about him until we did feel that he was an old friend whom we had known for years. I must, however, admit that, although he became completely real to us, we did tend to mould his character and history to suit our convenience.

As I have just related, we had decided that Major Martin was a rather brilliant officer and was trusted by his superiors: his only visible lapses were the all too common ones of having lost his identity card and having recently let his pass to Combined Operations H.Q. run out of date.

On that foundation we built a character which could be evidenced by documents in his pockets: that was the only means that we had whereby to convey his personality to the Germans.

We decided that he should be fond of a good time, so he could have an invitation to a night club; it was a probable result of a certain amount of extravagance that he would have a letter from his bank about his overdraft; he could have been staying at a Service club while in London, so he might have a receipted bill for the last part of his stay there. In this way he was developing from an abstraction into something rather more definite.

But how could we make him really "come to life"?

The only way to do it was by letting him carry in his pockets letters which would convey to the reader something really personal about him. On the other hand, if one were able to stop a passer-by in the street and search his pockets, it would be very seldom that one would hit on any occasion when he had letters about him which covered more than trivial details. When we approached our problem in that way, we came to the conclusion that the only times when a man is certain to be carrying "live" letters conveying a vivid picture of him and his life would be when he had recently become engaged and was carrying love letters on him and making arrangements for married life. We therefore decided that "a marriage should be arranged" between Bill Martin and some girl just before he was sent abroad.

So Major Martin "met" a charming girl called Pam early in April, became engaged to her almost at once (those wartime courtships!); she gave him a snap of herself and he gave her an engagement ring; he had a couple of ecstatic letters from her, one written when staying away the weekend and one written in the office (while her boss was out) in an agony of emotion, as he had hinted that he was being sent abroad somewhere. He would have with him the bill for the engagement ring—unpaid of course, as he had an overdraft to deal with. Lastly, he could have an old-fashioned father who disapproved of war weddings and who would insist on his son making a will if he persisted in so foolish and improvident a step.

We felt that we could not hope to build up a personality more definitely than that with only a pocketful of letters—but they had to sound genuine and they had to be written by someone. We could, of course, have written them ourselves—most of us knew only too well what a letter about an overdraft looked like, and some of us had made wills or received love letters, but I thought it best to rely on the expert hand so that there could be no possibility of any mistake.

Some of the items were easy. For instance, one of our number had an invitation to the Cabaret Club with no name on it, so the night club was easily provided for. The letter about the overdraft was only slightly more difficult. Through another of our number we got a letter from Lloyds Bank dated the 14th April calling on Major Martin to pay off an overdraft of some £79. I was asked, later on, whether it was usual for a letter dealing with such a comparatively small sum to have been signed by the Joint General Manager at Head Office; I had already considered this, as I know from bitter experience that such letters are usually signed by the branch manager. When I raised this question at the time, I was assured that, although it was true that such letters were more usually signed by the manager of the appropriate branch, it did quite often happen that the letter would come from Head Office in certain circumstances. As the officer concerned in getting this letter had a "lead in" to the Head Office, it was decided to use that: I did not think that the Germans would have had the experience that we had had of overdrafts and, after all, even if the amount was small, Major Martin's father was clearly a man of some importance. This letter was drafted for us personally by Mr. E. Whitley Jones, the Joint General Manager of Lloyds Bank, typed in his office and signed by him. It read as follows:

Lloyds Bank Limited
Head Office
London, E.C.3.

Private   14th April, 1943.
Major W. Martin, R.M.,

Army and Navy Club,
Pall Mall,
London, S.W.1.

DEAR SIR,

I am given to understand that in spite of repeated application your overdraft amounting to £79. 19*s*. 2*d*. still outstands.

In the circumstances, I am now writing to inform you that unless this amount, plus interest at 4% to date of payment, is received forthwith we shall have no alterna-

tive but to take the necessary steps to protect our in-
terests.

Yours faithfully,
(*Signed*) E. WHITLEY JONES,
Joint General Manager.

It had been arranged that this letter from the bank
should be sent through the post to Major Martin
at the Naval and Military Club, but it was errone-
ously posted addressed to him at the Army and Navy
Club, Pall Mall; there the Hall Porter marked the
envelope "Not known at this address" and added
"Try Naval and Military Club, 94 Piccadilly." This
seemed to us to be a most convincing indication
that the letter was real and not specially prepared,
so we decided that Major Martin should keep this
letter in its envelope.

One of us had got the co-operation of the Naval
and Military Club; we had been given a bill dated
the 24th April which showed that Major Martin had
been a temporary member of that club and had
stayed there for the nights of the 18th to 23rd April
inclusive; apart from its other purpose of general
build-up of the Major's personality, it afforded a
strong indication that he was still in London on the
24th.

Similarly, there was but little difficulty in getting
the bill for the engagement ring. I chose S. J. Phil-
lips, the Bond Street jewellers, as I knew that they

had an international trade, so that it was probable
that there would be bill-heads of theirs available in
Germany to prove, if comparison were to be made,
how genuine Major Martin's bill was. That bill was
dated the 19th April, but showed that the ring had
actually been bought on the 15th.

We were in some difficulty in getting these and
the other documents. Obviously, the true story of
why we wanted them could not be told, but I was
convinced that just to ask for them and to give no
reason, except that it was for something secret, was
liable to cause talk; on the other hand, once a plausible reason was given we felt sure that we could
rely on those whom we approached.

So my "cover story" was that there was someone
who seemed suspiciously interested in officers who
were temporarily hard up: we wanted to have some
documents, building up towards a shortage of money,
which a particular person could leave about his
rooms where they would be seen by this individual.
We could then observe what his conduct was. This
seemed to be a satisfying story, and we received
ready help—and no one ever let us down with the
slightest leak.

What might be called the supporting cast among
the documents having been provided for, we now
had to obtain the "stars."

First of all we needed a suitable snapshot of Pam,
Major Martin's fiancée. The scheme which we de-

vised was to ask the more attractive girls in our various offices to lend us a snapshot of themselves for use in a photographic identity parade—the sort of thing where the photographs of one or two suspects are shuffled in among those of a number of perfectly innocent persons and the "witness" is asked to pick out the one of the person whom he had seen; we asked for a variegated lot, and got quite a collection. We eventually chose a charming photograph and returned the remainder. The subject of the photograph was working in the War Office and, as she had access to "Top Secret" papers, we were able to tell her that we wanted to use the photograph as that of someone's fictitious fiancée in a deception, and she gave her permission.

None of us had felt up to writing the love letters —after all, ours was not the feminine point of view —and it was a bit difficult to ask a girl whether she could write a first-rate pæan of love. So we asked a girl working in one of the offices whether she could get some girl to do it. She took on the job, but never would tell us the name of the girl who produced the two magnificent letters that Major Martin was to carry with him.

I had decided that the first of these should be written on my brother-in-law's notepaper, for I was sure that no German could resist the "Englishness" of such an address as "The Manor House, Ogbourne St. George, Marlborough, Wiltshire"; this letter, dated "Sunday 18th," ran as follows:

The Manor House,
Ogbourne St. George,
Marlborough, Wiltshire.
Telephone: Ogbourne St. George 242.
Sunday, 18th.

I do think dearest that seeing people like you off at railway stations is one of the poorer forms of sport. A train going out can leave a howling great gap in ones life & one has to try madly—& quite in vain—to fill it with all the things one used to enjoy a whole five weeks ago. That lovely golden day we spent together—oh! I know it has been said before, but if *only* time could sometimes stand still just for a *minute*—But that line of thought is too pointless. Pull your socks up Pam & dont be a silly little fool.

Your letter made me feel slightly better—but I shall get horribly conceited if you go on saying things like that about me—they're utterly unlike ME, as I'm afraid you'll soon find out. Here I am for the weekend in this divine place with Mummy & Jane being too sweet & understanding the whole time, bored beyond words & panting for Monday so that I can get back to the old grindstone again. What an idiotic waste!

Bill darling, do let me know as soon as you get fixed & can make some more plans, & dont *please* let them send you off into the blue the horrible way they do nowadays—now that we've found each other out of the whole world, I dont think I could bear it—

All my love,
PAM.

It was followed by two sheets of plain paper, such

as was used in Government offices for carbon copies; the letter was headed "Office, Wednesday, 21st," and the writing, which started reasonably good, suddenly degenerated into a scrawl as the letter was hastily brought to an end when the writer's boss was heard returning. It ran:

Office.
Wednesday, 21st.

The Bloodhound has left his kennel for half an hour so here I am scribbling nonsense to you again. Your letter came this morning just as I was dashing out—madly late as usual! You do write such heavenly ones. But what are these horrible dark hints you're throwing out about being sent off somewhere—*of course* I won't say a word to anyone—I never do when you tell me things, but it's not abroad is it? Because I won't have it, I won't, tell them so from me. Darling, why did we go and meet in the middle of a war, such a silly thing for anybody to do—if it weren't for the war we might have been nearly married by now, going round together choosing curtains etc. And I wouldn't be sitting in a dreary Government office typing idiotic minutes all day long—I *know* the futile sort of work I do doesn't make the war one minute shorter—

Dearest Bill, I'm so thrilled with my ring—scandalously extravagant—you know how I adore diamonds—I simply can't stop looking at it.

I'm going to a rather dreary dance tonight with Jock & Hazel, I think they've got some other man coming. You know what their friends always turn out to be like, he'll have the sweetest little Adam's apple & the shiniest bald head! How beastly & ungrateful of me, but it isn't really that—you know—don't you?

Look darling, I've got next Sunday & Monday off for Easter. I shall go home for it of course, *do* come too if you possibly can, or even if you can't get away from London I'll dash up and we'll have an evening of gaiety —(By the way Aunt Marian said to bring you to dinner next time I was up, but I think that might wait?)

Here comes the Bloodhound, masses of love & a kiss

from

PAM.

We felt that we had been well served, and that the letters were ideal for our purpose.

To take the part of Major Martin's father we chose a young wartime officer who produced a brilliant tour de force; the letter of the 13th April and the enclosure seemed to me to be so redolent of Edwardian pomposity that no one *could* have invented them—no one but a father of the old school could have written them. The letter and its enclosure read:

Tel. No. 98.   Black Lion Hotel,
                                                           Mold,
                                                                  N. Wales.
                                                    13*th April,* 1943.

MY DEAR WILLIAM,

I cannot say that this Hotel is any longer as comfortable as I remember it to have been in pre-war days. I am, however, staying here as the only alternative to imposing myself once more upon your aunt whose depleted staff & strict regard for fuel economy (which I agree to be necessary in wartime) has made the house almost uninhabitable to a guest, at least one of my age. I propose to be in Town for the nights of the 20th & 21st of April when no doubt we shall have an opportunity to meet. I enclose the copy of a letter which I have written to Gwatkin of McKenna's about your affairs. You will see that I have asked him to lunch with me at the Carlton Grill (which I understand still to be open) at a quarter to one on Wednesday the 21st. I should be glad if you would make it possible to join us. We shall not however wait luncheon for you, so I trust that, if you are able to come, you will make a point of being punctual.

Your cousin Priscilla has asked to be remembered to you. She has grown into a sensible girl though I cannot say that her work for the Land Army has done much to improve her looks. In that respect I am afraid that she will take after her father's side of the family.

Your affectionate

FATHER

Copy
Tel. No. 98.

Black Lion Hotel,
Mold,
N. Wales.
10th April.

MY DEAR GWATKIN,

I have considered your recent letter concerning the Settlement which I intend to make on the occasion of William's marriage. The provisions which you outline ap-

pear to me reasonable except in one particular. Since in
this case the wife's family will not be contributing to the
settlement I do not think it proper that they should necessarily preserve, after William's death, a life interest in
the funds which I am providing. I should agree to this
course only were there children of the marriage. Will
you therefore so redraft the Settlement as to provide that
if there are children the income is paid to the wife
only until such time as she remarries or the children
come of age. After that date the children alone should
benefit.

I intend to be in London for the two nights of the 20th
& 21st of April. I should be glad if you could make it
convenient to take luncheon with me at the Carlton Grill
at a quarter to one on Wednesday 21st. If you will bring
the new draft with you we shall have leisure to examine
it afterwards. I have written to William & hope that he
will be able to join us.

Yrs. sincerely,
(*Signed*) J. G. MARTIN.

F. A. S. Gwatkin, Esq.,
McKenna & Co.,
14 Waterloo Place,
London, S.W.1.

We selected the Black Lion Hotel, Mold, not only
because it also seemed so British an address that it
in itself conveyed an impression of truth, but it was
also consistent with Major Martin's birthplace of
Cardiff; I hope that they will forgive us for taking
and using their notepaper—and especially for ques-

tioning the comfort for which that hotel is noted.

Finally, I got a friend who was a partner in the firm to round off the picture by drafting the following letter, and writing it on McKenna & Co.'s note-paper:

McKenna & Co.   14, Waterloo Place,
Solicitors.   London, S.W.1.
                    Our ref.: McL/EG
                                        19*th April,* 1943.
DEAR SIR,
                    Re your affairs

We thank you for your letter of yesterday's date re-turning the draft of your will approved. We will insert the legacy of £50 to your batman and our Mr. Gwatkin will bring the fair copy with him when he meets you at lunch on the 21st inst. so that you can sign it there.

The inspector of taxes has asked us for particulars of your service pay and allowances during 1941/2 before he will finally agree to the amount of reliefs due to you for that year. We cannot find that we have ever had these particulars and shall, therefore, be grateful if you will let us have them.

                            Yours faithfully,
                                    MCKENNA & CO.

Major W. Martin, R.M.,
Naval & Military Club,
94, Piccadilly,
London, W.1.

When we read all those documents together they conveyed to us the impression of a real person—of a real person who lived—of a man who really was. We did not feel that more could be done with the few papers that a man could reasonably have in his pocket.

However, we took some precautions before we gave the letters to Major Martin. The letters, other than the love letters, I carried in my pocket for the appropriate number of days to get them into the right condition. But the love letters were more of a problem, especially as one of them was on flimsy paper. It was obvious that they would have been read and re-read and would not be in mint condition, but the proper appearance could not be produced quickly by scrumpling them up and then smoothing them out again (as someone foolishly suggested would be the suitable method); once a piece of paper has been scrumpled no amount of flattening will erase the fact that it has been treated that way—and the one thing that Bill Martin would never have done to those letters was to crush them up. So I did what he would have done; I folded and unfolded the letters again and again, and in addition I rubbed them carefully on my clothing to get a little patina on to them.

7.

MAJOR MARTIN GETS READY FOR WAR

W E HAD GONE steadily on with our preparations although final approval for the launching of the operation had not yet been obtained.

After considering Sir Archibald Nye's letter, the Chiefs of Staff had given approval in principle; we now pressed for authority to start. There was bound to be a conflict of interest at this stage: the Chiefs of Staff were naturally reluctant to become committed to the Germans receiving the information contained in the letter as our strategy *might* be changed—if that had happened it would not have been for the first time! On the other hand, we simply *had* to get the letter to Spain by the beginning of May if the operation was to be of any value; we had to give the German Intelligence Service time to get the information, convince themselves of its genuineness by any check-up that they might want, and then to "appreciate" it and pass the result on to the Operational Staff. The latter would then need time to make their arrangements and to send their forces to the wrong places—and, if we wanted them not to fortify Sicily, it was no good waiting until those fortifications were complete.

The Chiefs of Staff accepted this necessity and gave their final approval, subject to reference to the Prime Minister, to whom the matter was submitted through General Ismay.

When the Prime Minister was told that there was some risk of pinpointing Sicily, if the operation went wrong, he replied (as I have already recorded), "I don't see that that matters. Anybody but a damn' fool would *know* it is Sicily." We felt that he ought also to be informed that our efforts might be wasted, as there was always the chance that the body *might* be recovered by a Spaniard who was not co-operating with the Germans and the papers might be returned to us intact. The Prime Minister realized that that risk was not great either, and disposed of this point with a grin and a chuckle, saying, "I don't see that that matters either. We can always try again!"

So we had received the all-clear, subject to General Eisenhower being informed of the plan. If he had had any objection, or any change of strategy had occurred before the body was actually launched, the operation could have been cancelled in the way I had provided in paragraph 8 of the "operation orders" to Lieutenant Jewell.

Meanwhile we had to undertake the least pleasant part of our work—we had to get the body ready for its mission.

We heartily disliked this task. In spite of the great service which we were confident that the body would render to its country, it went against the grain to disturb its rest; in addition, there was an odd psychological reaction on each occasion that we saw the body lying stiff and cold. By this time Major Martin had become a completely living person for us; we felt that we knew him just as one knows one's best friend. After all, one has to be very close to a friend to read his love letters and the very personal letters that he gets from his father; we had come to feel that we had known Bill Martin from his early childhood and were taking a genuine and personal interest in the progress of his courtship and financial troubles. I had thought that I might say that we, who had created him, knew him as a father knows his son—but that would have been inaccurate. We knew him far better than most fathers know their sons; so as to create him we had had to make ourselves know his every thought and his probable reaction to any event that might occur in his life.

So we never relished the prospect of a visit to the place where the corpse was in cold storage—and George and I had to pay no less than three visits to him. First we had to disturb him to try to get a suitable photograph, and we took that opportunity to check his measurements, and especially the size that he took in boots. Then we thought it wise to pay a second visit and dress him so that he was fully ready for his journey in case there was any hitch which could not be rectified in haste. And it was a good thing that we did, for we had forgotten one point.

I have used the expression "lying stiff and cold." We had realized that it would be difficult to dress a body fully, from the underwear up, when it was in such a condition; we had checked on the situation when we took the photographs and found that, although difficult, it was possible. But we had forgotten the boots!

To appreciate what we were up against, it would be necessary for you to try to put a pair of boots on your feet, keeping your ankle and foot absolutely rigid, and with the latter at right angles to the leg—the operation is utterly impossible.

This was a bad check: we knew that to freeze and then to thaw a body, and then to freeze it again is a sure way to hasten the process of decomposition when eventually the body is allowed finally to thaw out. If we had to do this we might well vitiate the whole basis of Sir Bernard Spilsbury's calculations. What were we to do?

Suddenly we thought of the solution. We got an electric fire and thawed the feet and ankles only; then hurriedly, yet carefully, we dressed the body completely, and finally, with sincere mental apologies for what we were doing to it, replaced it in the cold storage.

Our third visit was on Saturday the 17th April, 1943 at 6 p.m., when we went to fetch Major Martin for the start of his journey. First we put the personal letters and the wallet with his passes and so on into his pockets. Then we added the usual "junk" that a man carries about on him, or unwittingly collects in his pockets. The final list was somewhat impressive:

Identity discs (2) "Major W. MARTIN, R.M., R/C," attached to braces.
Silver cross on silver chain round neck.
Watch, wrist.
Wallet, containing:
    Photograph of fiancée.
    Book of stamps (2 used).
    2 letters from fiancée.
    St. Christopher plaque.
    Invitation to Cabaret Club.
    C.C.O. Pass   } in cellophane
    Admiralty Identity Card } container.
    Torn-off top of letter.

1 £5 note—5th March, 1942 $\frac{227}{C}$ 45827.

3 £1 notes X34D527008
                    W21D029293
                    X66D443119

1 half-crown.
2 shillings.
2 sixpences.
4 pennies.
Letter from "Father."
Letter from "Father" to McKenna & Co., solicitors.
Letter from Lloyds Bank.
Letter from McKenna & Co., solicitors.
Bill (receipted) from Naval and Military Club.
Bill (cash) from Gieves Ltd.
Bill for engagement ring.
2 bus tickets.
2 counterfoil stubs of tickets for Prince of Wales'
     Theatre, 22nd April, 1943.
Box of matches.
Packet of cigarettes.
Bunch of keys.
Pencil stub.

I must digress here to explain the item "2 counterfoil stubs of tickets for Prince of Wales' Theatre,
22nd April, 1943." As I have said, it was on the
17th April that we went to fetch Major Martin, and
he was to sail on the 19th; he was due to be
launched into the sea off Huelva on about the
29th or 30th April. On the other hand, if he had

been travelling by air, as we wanted the Germans to
believe, the journey would only have taken a single
day. When we considered this difference in time, we
decided to work the time-table back the other way:
if we deducted from the arrival in Huelva on about
the 30th April some five or six days in which the
body might have been drifting ashore from an aircraft which had come to grief out at sea (we had
reckoned that the eventual degree of decomposition
would probably support an immersion of about that
period), that would mean that Major Martin would
have left London on about the 24th of April, and for
that reason the bill for his room at the Naval and
Military Club was dated that day. But here George
had another of his brilliant ideas; it suddenly came
into his ingenious mind that anyone who sees the
stub of a theatre ticket at once assumes that the
ticket has been used, but there was no reason why
we should not buy theatre tickets valid for any date
after the body had in fact left London, and then
tear off the stubs and waste the tickets. So we decided that Bill Martin and Pam should have a
farewell party before he left; we felt that they
would enjoy the Sid Fields show at the Prince of
Wales' Theatre, and we bought four tickets for that
show (the reason why we bought four will be related later), tore off the stubs of two and put them
into Major Martin's pocket. Once again a small de-

tail was to play its part in the deception, and this afterthought "went home" whereas the bill for the room at the Club was overlooked by the Spaniards and Germans.

Finally, we added the briefcase containing the important documents, and here we made a slight alteration from our intended arrangements of which I had notified Lieutenant Jewell. We had intended to take the briefcase up to the Clyde separately from the canister and give it into Lieutenant Jewell's care, but when it came to the point we found that the bag could be inserted into the canister with the body; and we therefore took this course, as it was an obvious safeguard against any forgetfulness during the launching of the body off Huelva. Lieutenant Jewell would have a difficult task, especially if it was rough, and his mind would be fully occupied with that and the safety of his ship: it would have been a pity if Major Martin had floated ashore while his briefcase remained in Lieutenant Jewell's safe.

When we had completed the clothing, filled all the pockets and attached the briefcase, we wrapped the body in a blanket so as to prevent it getting rubbed during its journey. When we had arrived we had stood the canister up on end and filled it with dry ice; when this had melted, we refilled the canister and again waited for the ice to melt. Then we lifted Major Martin and reverently and carefully lowered

him into the canister and packed him round with
still more dry ice. Finally, we put on the lid and
screwed down the nuts. Major Martin was ready to
go to war.

8

THE
JOURNEY
NORTH

Oᴜʀ ᴘᴀʀᴛʏ ᴄᴏɴsɪsᴛᴇᴅ of George and myself, together with Jock Horsfall, the racing motorist,
who was on special duty with the War Office, one of
whose 30-cwt. Ford vans we had borrowed—and, of
course, Major Martin in his canister.

The journey nearly ended almost before it had
started for, as we drove out from the "cold storage"
to start back to George's flat in London, we caught
sight of a queue waiting to see a spy film at the
local cinema; the same thought flashed into each of
our minds: what would those people think if we were
to stop and say to them, "Don't bother about the
film. We can tell you a much better story—and ours
is true. Just look inside this canister"? And we all

burst out laughing to such an extent that Jock almost rammed a tram-standard.

But we got safely back to George's flat. There we cooked ourselves some dinner and ate it, taking turns to keep an eye on the van outside; if a thief had got away with the canister, he would have had a disappointment—and a shock—when he opened it, but his disappointment would have been nothing to ours. So we made ourselves some sandwiches and filled thermos flasks as we realized that we could not leave the van during the journey north.

Our preparations completed, we set off for Greenock, Jock and I taking it in turns to drive. It was a long and tiring journey, as we could, of course, only use masked headlights; at one point we drove straight across a "roundabout" which, fortunately, only had smooth grass in its center once we had mounted the curb. The sound of aircraft overhead added to our worries; for although the *Seraph* was not due to sail until the 19th and we had got a fair amount of time in hand in which to cope, without any really serious consequences, with any traffic diversions through bomb damage, Lieutenant Jewell had asked that we should arrive before midday on the 18th, in case there were any last-minute difficulties in stowing the canister. However, we did not crash the van and, as far as I know, all the aircraft were friendly, so we drove on through the night, taking it in turns to sleep on the floor of the van.

Early on the morning of the 18th we arrived at Greenock and drove to the dock, where we had arranged to meet the launch that was to ferry us out to H.M.S. *Forth*, the submarine depot ship lying in the Holy Loch.

Here we ran up against a snag. I had visualized that there might be some difficulty in lowering the canister into the launch, so I had carefully said in the signal from D.N.I. arranging for our arrival that I would have "one, repeat one" package weighing over 400 pounds and requesting assistance in embarking it. In spite of that particularity, the signal had been read as if our total baggage weighed 400 pounds in several packages. As a result, we found ourselves faced with a launch surging up and down some feet below the quay and the "party" for which we had asked consisted of one rating. He was very obliging, but no rope was available and to lower the canister without disaster was clearly impossible.

Anticipating all sorts of trouble and delay before I, a complete stranger, could arrange for a party to be got together, I hurried off to the Flag Officer in Charge's headquarters—and my luck still held. The Duty Officer on duty turned out to be a Wren who had been serving as a rating in the signal office at Hull when I was on the Staff there. We greeted one another as old friends and, all difficulties having been quickly smoothed out, I returned to the dock with half a dozen ratings and some rope with which to lower the canister.

We were soon ferried down to H.M.S. *Forth,* where I handed Major Martin over to Lieutenant Jewell. I also gave him the rubber dinghy which he was to launch with the body; so as to give the impression of an accident and haste, the dinghy was to be launched upside down, and it seemed better to leave only one of the collapsible aluminum oars in it; I therefore kept the other one, and I still have it as a souvenir. As it turned out, however, the launching of the dinghy made no difference; a body might be of no value to a Spanish fisherman, but a rubber dinghy certainly was—so ours was never heard of again. I hope the finder made good use of it.

We had been advised that, if a Catalina flying boat sank out at sea, it was unlikely that any wreckage would float ashore, so we did not provide Lieutenant Jewell with anything more with which to simulate signs of a disaster.

The canister was duly stowed on board H.M.S. *Seraph* and I had final discussions with Lieutenant Jewell. In these I suggested that he might be able to launch the body with only officers present on deck. If he could, it would reduce the number of persons who were "in the know" and thus make leakage of the story less likely—and it was more than usually important to guard against leakage, as the story of the launching of a dead body off the coast of Spain was one that would tempt the best of us to gossip.

If he could launch the body in this way, he would obviously need a "cover story" for the rest of the crew, who would see a package that they had thought to be destined for Malta taken up on deck off the coast of Spain, after which it would never reappear. I suggested that he might tell them that the so-called optical instruments were, in fact, a secret weather-reporting buoy and that, if the Spaniards learned of its existence, they would remove it. If he had to have the crew on deck during the launching, either because of rough weather or for any other reason, he would use the cover story that I had given him in the "operation orders."

All went well with our arrangements, and on our return to London we were able to end our report with the statement: "On April 19th, 1943 at 1800 British Double Summer Time H.M. s/m *Seraph* sailed from Holy Loch." Remembering the nature of the cargo, I felt that these names were most suitable and augured well for the success of the operation.

9.

THE
LAUNCHING
OF
THE
BODY

THERE THEN CAME a period of anxiety; I had never
had any qualms about the success of the operation,
but now that its execution was out of my hands I
kept thinking of things that might go wrong. Oddly
enough, I still did not worry whether the Germans
would see through the deception. I was confident
that they would not. My anxiety was confined to the
launching of the body. Could we really be sure that
the body would float ashore or would I have to confess, after all the effort, that the whole thing was a
complete flop? And, in my worst moments, I visualized the *Seraph* getting into trouble off Huelva,
where she had gone only because of my plan. Still,
I had more than enough to do with my other duties
not to have much time for worry, and we did have

at least one very cheerful evening during this period.

It had seemed absurd to waste the tickets, the stubs of which Major Martin had in his pocket. So we had, as I have recorded, bought four tickets, and we took care to give Major Martin the stubs of the middle two seats of the four.

George and I then invited "Pam" and Jill, the girl who had arranged for the writing of the love letters, to "Bill Martin's farewell party." We started at the Prince of Wales' Theatre, where the manager let us in after he had inspected the block of tickets and we had explained that someone had torn the stubs off the center pair "as a joke"—we did not tell him that the joke was on the Germans.

After the theatre we went on to the Gargoyle Club for dinner. There we were shown to one of the side tables which had a banquette faced by two chairs. I suggested that the two girls should take the more comfortable banquette, but Jill turned to George and said, "Considering Bill and Pam are engaged, they are the least affectionate couple I know. They don't even want to sit together at his farewell party before he goes abroad." At this the couple at the next table looked round and pricked up their ears.

I "explained" to Jill that even if Pam and I were engaged we had only known one another for a few days (obvious disapproval of war weddings registered at the next table), and then added, as an afterthought, that it would be different when Pam and

I knew one another better, for my boss had said (in the letter that she had seen[1]) that, although I was quiet and shy at first, I really did know my stuff. At this the couple at the next table registered even stronger disapproval and got up and danced.

I might interpolate another result of this joking identification of Bill Martin with me. Pam followed it up by giving me a larger copy of the photograph that was on its way to Spain in Bill Martin's wallet, and signed it "Till death do us part. Your loving Pam"—a safe inscription, as "I" was already "dead." At that time I was staying with my mother, and to see her reaction I put the photograph on my dressing table. I was disappointed—she said nothing. About a year later, when my wife returned from America, where she had been doing a job in our Security Co-ordination Service, I showed her the photograph, and she astonished me by saying, "So *that* was why your mother started writing in her letters that she felt that I should come home as soon as my job allowed it"!

While we were waiting in London, the *Seraph* was having an uneventful passage to the coast of Spain. The first news that we got was from the pre-arranged signal which informed us, on the 30th April, that "Operation Mincemeat" had been completed. This

[1] Lord Louis Mountbatten's letter to Admiral Cunningham.

was followed by a letter sent by Lieutenant Jewell
from Gibraltar:

Most Secret and Personal

From: The Commanding Officer, H.M. Submarine *Seraph.*
Date: 30th April, 1943.
To Director of Naval Intelligence.
Copy to F.O.S.
(for Lt.-Cdr. The Hon. E. E. S. Montagu, R.N.V.R.)
  personal.

Operation Mincemeat

Weather: The wind was variable altering between
S.W. and S.E., force 2. It was expected that the sea
breeze would spring up in the morning, close inshore, as
it had on the previous morning in similar conditions.

Sea and swell—2:0—Sky overcast with very low clouds
—visibility was patchy, 1 to 2 miles—Barometer 1016.

2. *Fishing Boats:* A large number of small fishing
boats were working in the bay. The closest was left,
about a mile off, and it is not thought that the submarine
was observed by them.

3. *Operation:* The time of 0430 was chosen as being
the nearest to Low Water Lisbon (0731), which would
allow the submarine to be well clear by dawn. The canister was opened at 0415 and the body extracted. The
blanket was opened up and the body examined. The brief
case was found to be securely attached. . . . The "Mae
West" was blown up very hard and no further air was
needed. The body was placed in the water at 0430 in a
position 148° Portil Pillar 1.3 miles approximately eight
cables from the beach and started to drift inshore. This

was aided by the wash of the screws going full speed astern. The rubber dinghy was placed in the water blown up and upside down about half a mile further south of this position. The submarine then withdrew to seaward and the canister, filled with water and containing the blanket, tapes and also the rubber dingy's container, was pushed over the side in position 36°37′30 North 07°18′00 West in 310 fathoms of water by sounding machine. The container would not at first submerge, but after being riddled by fire from Vickers gun and also .455 revolver at very short range was seen to sink. Signal reporting operation complete was passed at 0715.

A sample of the water close inshore is attached.

N. A. JEWELL,
Lieutenant-in-Command.

This letter included a description of the condition of the body; there was rather more decomposition than we had expected (perhaps due to oxygen trapped in the clothing and blanket), but not more than was to be expected had the body been floating half immersed in the sea for some days.

Later on I got a more detailed account from a member of the ship's company—I got it at second-hand and, as my go-between was a journalist by profession, the picture that is conjured up by his account is much more vivid than anything that I could record. I therefore give it just as I received it:

As the *Seraph* slid from the shadow of her depot ship

and down the Clyde, the commander—he was only twenty-nine—saluted from the conning tower, then went below.

Of the five officers and fifty ratings on board, only he knew the secret of his odd piece of cargo.

Wisecracks

The cylindrical metal canister now rested in a forward chamber of the submarine.

Because of its weight and shape, the six ratings who maneuvered it into place joked about "John Brown's body." And there was many a wisecrack about "our new shipmate, Charlie."

Today, ten years later, those fifty ex-members of the Seraph's crew will be shaken to learn how close to the truth they were.

They had been told in the briefing for the trip that the metal canister contained a secret weather-reporting device to be floated experimentally off the coast of Spain. It was actually marked "Handle with Care—Optical Instruments—for special F.O.S. shipment."

For ten days the Seraph sailed and her crew saw nothing of the sun. Surfacing at night, she was off Huelva, on the southwest coast of Spain, undetected and according to schedule, on April 30.

The spot selected for floating "Major Martin" ashore was 1,600 yards off the mouth of the Huelva river.

In the afternoon the Seraph ventured an inshore reconnaissance. The periscope revealed a fishing fleet of about fifty vessels. But the prevailing mist and a mile detour helped the submarine to escape detection. Then she went back to the sea bed for the rest of the day.

Mysterious

Zero hour was 4.30 in the morning. When the *Seraph* surfaced again it was dark as pitch. The new moon had set and the ebb tide was just on the turn.

Through the conning tower went the five officers, and the submarine was trimmed down until an inch of the calm sea lapped over the casing. The mysterious canister was hauled aloft.

Only then, with all ratings below, did Lieutenant Jewell let his officers into the secret. Lieutenant Jewell told them that the canister at their feet contained a corpse. The operation, he said, was part of an Allied plan to deceive the enemy into drawing his defensive forces away from the spot selected for the main thrust of the Mediterranean invasion.

Phoney invasion plans were to be "planted" on the enemy through the medium of the body of this man purporting to be "Major Martin," victim of an air crash at sea.

Huelva had been chosen for the "plant" because it was known that the German agent there was being well fed with military intelligence by local collaborators.

What a story to be sprung on you suddenly in the middle of the night with the Atlantic lapping round your boots. But if the junior officers were shaken by their commander's dramatic and gruesome revelation, they did not betray it.

Only reaction was the comment from one of them: "Isn't it pretty unlucky carrying dead bodies around?"

Tension

Then quickly and quietly the five set about their task. While three kept watch, the other helped Lieutenant Jewell to unlock the bolts of the canister with the spanner attached to the case. Ten minutes they worked before the lid came away.

Then the blanketed body was slid gently from its vacuum coffin. For a moment the tension was relieved as the officers stiffened with silent respect in the presence of death.

On his knees again, Lieutenant Jewell plucked at knotted tapes and the blanket fell away.

There followed the final check. Were the Major's uniform and badges intact? Was his hand gripping the handle of the all-important despatch case? Was the case securely strapped to his belt?

Everything in order, Jewel bent low to inflate the Major's "Mae West."

Only one thing remained—though it was not in the routine instructions. Four young officers bent bare heads in simple tribute as their commander murmured what prayers he could remember from the Burial Service.

For them, sworn to secrecy, these words from Psalm 39 held a special significance:

"I will keep my mouth as it were with a bridle: while the ungodly is in my sight. I held my tongue and spake nothing: I kept silence, yea, even from good words; but it was pain and grief to me."

A gentle push and the unknown warrior was drifting inshore with the tide on his last, momentous journey. "Major Martin" had gone to the war.

The risk that Lieutenant Jewell had taken in going so close to the shore had given us every possible chance of success. We could now only wait to see how Major Martin would carry out *his* part of the job.

10.

MAJOR MARTIN LANDS IN SPAIN

ON THE 3rd MAY we received a signal from the Naval Attaché in Madrid. He had been informed by the Vice-Consul at Huelva that the body of a Major Martin, Royal Marines, had been picked up just off-shore by a fisherman on the 30th April. The body had been duly handed over to the Vice-Consul and had been given a full military funeral, at which the Spanish Services and civilian authorities were represented, at twelve noon on the following day in the cemetery at Huelva. There was no mention in the Attaché's message of the black official briefcase or of any official papers.

There then followed an exchange of signals between the Admiralty and the Naval Attaché. If the papers had been what they purported to be, it was

obvious that, when the death of Major Martin and
the arrival of his body in Spain became known at
Combined Operations H.Q., there would have been
a realization of the fact that a most secret document
had gone astray, and reference to Sir Archibald Nye
would have revealed the full measure of the disas-
trous "leak" of strategic information that might have
taken place. In those circumstances, increasingly
pressing messages would have been sent to the Naval
Attaché, urging him to try to get the documents
back at all costs, but warning him that he must take
the utmost care not to show undue anxiety lest that
should alert the Spaniards to the importance of the
documents and encourage them to open or "lose"
them. We naturally had to act as if the whole affair
was genuine, and the signals were therefore on those
lines.

We started by a signal on the 4th May stating that
Major Martin had some papers with him which were
of great secrecy and importance, and instructing the
Attaché to make a formal demand for them. If they
were not forthcoming, he should make very discreet
but searching inquiries at Huelva to see if they had
been washed ashore and, if so, what had happened
to them. If he did recover them, he was to signal to
"D.N.I.—Personal" the names of the addresses; he
was not to open the envelopes, but to return them
as quickly as possible to D.N.I.

We followed that by another signal informing him

that it had been ascertained that there were three letters, of the utmost importance, and that they were believed to be in a black official briefcase with the Royal cypher on it. He was again warned on no account to arouse the interest of the Spaniards in the documents.

We learned from the Attaché, in reply to the first signal, that the Minister of Marine had informed him, in answer to a studiously routine inquiry, that the documents had been passed through "Naval channels" and would only reach Madrid via the Spanish Naval H.Q. at Cadiz. This would take some days. The Attaché had learned that the Vice-Consul at Huelva had had no opportunity to get the briefcase or other documents.

Then, on the 13th May, the Attaché informed us that the Spanish Chief of Naval Staff, in the absence of the Minister of Marine, who was away, had just given him all Major Martin's effects, including a black briefcase—the latter was open with a key in the lock. The Chief of Naval Staff had said that "everything was there," and the Naval Attaché had thanked him.

Although the Attaché had gained a strong impression that the Chief of Naval Staff knew at least something of the contents of the letters, he considered that there was no reason to think that that officer would divulge his knowledge to anyone. Of course, we did not suspect that officer of any breach of faith

—but if *he* knew of the contents it would be certain that others would also know. Things were going well —the "leak" was starting.

Our optimism was strengthened by the next message that we received from the Attaché. The Minister of Marine himself had referred to the papers when he saw the Attaché on Saturday, the 15th May. Apparently, he had heard, while in Valencia, that the papers had arrived in Madrid, and had immediately given orders to the Chief of Naval Staff to hand them over at once. He had done this lest someone might have had an unauthorized look at them, which might, he said, be a serious matter.

Nothing that had been said to the Minister of Marine before he left Madrid could have given rise to such anxiety about the documents, so we had no doubt at all that the envelopes must have been opened. That being the case, we were confident that there must be at any rate *one* Spaniard "in the know" who would pass the information on to the Germans. How close the co-operation was in fact we were not to learn until after the end of the war.

Meanwhile, discreet inquiries in Huelva filled in some of the details of what had happened. We learned with absolute certainty that a fisherman had noticed a floating object and had hailed a nearby launch, which took it on board. The object, which turned out to be the body of Major Martin, was landed on the nearest beach by the launch and handed over to an officer who happened to be exercising a detachment of infantry there.

A naval judicial officer was summoned, and he took charge of all the documents and personal effects. The body, after identification, was removed to the mortuary at Huelva for medical examination by a doctor, who certified that the man had fallen into the sea while still alive and had no bruises, and that death was due to asphyxiation, through immersion in the sea since five to eight days before. An American Air Force pilot who had crashed into the sea on the 27th April was then asked to inspect the body in case he could identify it, but he (naturally) could not do so.

The man whom we knew to be the chief German agent in the vicinity had soon learnt of the landing of the body. He quickly ascertained the details, including the names of the addressees of the letters in the briefcase, and had tried to get copies of all the documents, but he was not successful owing to the chance fact that, as the military patrol had been present to take charge of the body, the naval judicial officer had been called in, and neither he nor his associates had the right kind of contact with that particular official.

Although we were confident that all had gone well, we wanted a final check, and we waited impatiently for the return of the documents that Major Martin had carried; eventually they reached London and

were promptly submitted to scientific tests. Before
sending them out, we had taken precautions, which
I obviously cannot specify, which would help us to
check whether the envelopes had been tampered
with and, though the immersion in sea water made
certainty impossible, we were now able to say with
some degree of confidence from the physical evidence that the letters, or at least two of them, had
been removed from the envelopes, although the
seals appeared to be intact.

When we added this information to that which we
had received from Huelva and from the Naval Attaché, we were quite satisfied. There was little
doubt that the Spaniards had extracted the letters
and knew what was in them, and that the German
Intelligence Service knew of the important addressees; we could rely on the efficiency of the Germans to get all that they wanted out of that situation. We were sure that our confidence in the
Spanish end of the German Intelligence Service
would not be misplaced. It was now up to Berlin to
play *its* part.

Meanwhile, we must say farewell to Major Martin.
He had served his country well, and we felt that it
was up to us to see that his last resting-place should
be a fitting one and that proper tribute should be
paid to him, even if all this had to be done under
pseudonyms. We were glad to be able to show respect to him without any danger to the success of

the operation in which he had played so vital a part. Indeed, by doing what our instinct required of us, we would make it more difficult for the Germans to check the Spanish doctor's verdict—a verdict with which we were entirely satisfied. Frequent visits to the grave by British officials and their representatives would at least deter any exhumation by the Germans or Spaniards before the tombstone could be laid.

First of all we got the Naval Attaché to arrange for a wreath to be placed on the grave from Pam and the family; next we arranged that a tombstone should be laid as soon as possible and, finally, I wrote to the Naval Attaché, asking him to thank the Vice-Counsul at Huelva on behalf of Major Martin's family for all the trouble he had taken, and the consideration that had been shown, and asking also that photographs of the grave might be taken, as they would be treasured by the family and by Major Martin's fiancée, to whom he had so recently become engaged.

The wreath was composed of flowers from the garden of an English mining company at Huelva; the gravestone was of plain white marble and bore the inscription, "William Martin. Born 29th March, 1907. Died 24th April, 1943. Beloved son of John Glyndwyr Martin and the late Antonia Martin of Cardiff, Wales. *Dulce et decorum est pro patria mori.* R.I.P."

We could do no more for him, although we were

deeply in his debt and felt that very soon many thousands of his fellow countrymen and their American allies might owe their lives to him as they landed on the shores of Sicily. Indeed, my confidence in that probability was shared by now by those in authority: I had sent a message to Lieutenant Jewell to let him know that his part of the operation had been completely successful: as it was undesirable to send my message by signal, in case it aroused talk, I decided that Lieutenant Jewell would know what I meant when I wrote, "You will be pleased to learn that the Major is now very comfortable" on an ordinary picture postcard. But the Chiefs of Staff went one better; they sent a message to the Prime Minister, who was by then in Washington; it also had of necessity to be cryptic and read:

"Mincemeat Swallowed Whole."

11

WE
TIDY
UP
IN
ENGLAND

WE (and by this I mean all of us on the Allied side) had by now done our part of the job; if I may use a simile, we now had only to stone-wall, keeping our end up until close of play came with the landings in Sicily, leaving the Germans at the other end to do the scoring for us.

So, on the whole, we sat back and waited developments. However, as the days went by, we remembered that *The Times* used to reach Lisbon by air and the Germans might be keeping an eye on the casualty lists which were published from time to time. I therefore checked the average period that elapsed between a death and the subsequent announcement in the newspapers; it appeared as a general rule to be not more than about five weeks, and that, from the 24th April, would bring us to the first week of June.

Should we include Major Martin's name in such a list? Was it worth the complication involved? The landings in Sicily were planned for the second week in July, and the Germans could hardly be certain that the name of a genuine casualty would *have* to appear before then; and, if the deception had caused them to take any action, they would have done so before the first week of June and could hardly remedy any mistake—or even begin to do so —before we landed. On the other hand, it was always possible that the assault on Sicily might be delayed for some reason. After some hesitation, we decided that an omission to insert the name might do harm and that it was better to be sure than sorry.

Eventually, however, we were indeed sorry that we had added this embellishment to our creation, but fortunately only for the trouble that it gave us and not because it did any harm. As regards our objective of deception, all went smoothly and our phenomenal luck held. It was quite easy to get the Casualty Section of the Commissions and Warrants Branch of the Admiralty to accede to D.N.I.'s request that they should include the name of "Temporary Captain (Acting Major) William Martin, R.M." among the "Killed" in the next casualty list—I forget what explanation I gave when I conveyed the odd request. The announcement duly appeared in the issue of *The*

Times dated Friday, the 4th June, 1943. We will probably never know whether the Germans did in fact
spot this name, but, if they did, they would have
found, in the same list, the names of Rear-Admiral
P. J. Mack, D.S.O., and of Acting Captain Sir T. L.
Beevor, Bt., R.N. It had already been announced in
the newspapers that these two officers, with others
whose names had not been given, had died when an
airplane had been lost at sea. What could be more
plausible than that Major Martin had died with them
—and the fact that it was that list which happened to
be the next one was due to pure chance. It makes me
hope that the Germans *did* spot that list, as it would
be a pity if anything so artistic as that had been
wasted.

But it was then that trouble started over here;
casualty lists were studied by departments of whose
existence I was blissfully unaware and by others
whom I had forgotten. I was given a little experience
of the sort of trouble which I would have had on
a much larger scale had I allowed the messages passing between us and the Attaché in Madrid to have
the normal distribution.

The Naval Wills Department wanted to know
whether Major Martin had made a will—and if so,
where was it? The Medical Director-General's Department wanted to know whether Major Martin had
been killed in action, died of wounds, died on active

service, or what, so that their statistics could be kept in order.

Fortunately, the precautions that I had taken to ensure that any inquiries about Major Martin (or any of his documents) were adequately dealt with worked satisfactorily. I heard of these inquiries at a sufficiently early stage for me to be able to prevent their spreading too widely, but I had to deal with the departments concerned. I racked my brains what answer to give. I could not refer the Wills Department to McKenna & Co., the solicitors who had written to Major Martin about his will before he departed.

I had by now fully appreciated the truth of the aphorism, "Oh, what a tangled web we weave when first we practise to deceive," and was getting into the swing of it. I told the heads of each of those departments that they need not worry about Major Martin, or record him or his death. I explained that he was a special agent who had been sent on an important mission after having been given (with the First Sea Lord's authority) the cover of naval rank as an officer in the Royal Marines; after all, that account was perfectly true as far as it went. I only "forgot" to mention that he was already dead before any of that happened.

With D.N.I.'s authority, I impressed on them the vital need for secrecy, and they undertook to deal with the matter in their respective departments. The nearest we ever came to the operation "leaking" was over.

I might, perhaps, add that some years later, after I had been demobilized, people were still compiling other lists, and I suddenly got an urgent request to visit the Naval Intelligence Division. They had received other similar inquiries about Major Martin and wanted to know how I had dealt with such inquiries in the past, so that the same answer could be given again.

But apart from this matter of the casualty list, "Operation Mincemeat" was no longer in our hands. We had played our part and Lieutenant Jewell and Major Martin had played theirs. What were the Germans doing?

12.

THE
GERMAN
INTELLIGENCE
SERVICE
PLAYS
ITS
PART

THROUGH THE END OF MAY, through June and into July 1943 we had nothing on which to rely for our belief that we had succeeded in our plot, except for our faith in the thoroughness of the German penetration of Spain and the gullibility of the Germans. We were sure that we had succeeded in getting the documents to the Germans and that, now that we had achieved that first step, the picture presented to them was so complete and so authoritative that no Intelligence staff could fail to be certain that it had scored an epoch-making triumph.

We could picture the Intelligence chiefs rubbing their hands; they would be bound to preen themselves at the thought that the painstaking care and

efficiency with which they had built up their organization in Spain, and the liaison with important
Spanish officialdom, which was Admiral Canaris's [1]
special pride, had at last proved its worth. In the past
that organization must have provided Berlin with much
information about ship movements through the Straits
of Gibraltar as well as intelligence gained in the
British Isles and America and transmitted through
Madrid, but that was to be expected of any such
service. Besides, it had clearly been badly at fault
before the assault on North Africa, when, so far as
we could judge, the Germans had been taken by surprise. Now, at last, it had scored a real triumph.

To be able to provide the Operational Staff with
an exact copy of a letter from a Vice-Chief of a
General Staff to the Commander of an army in the
field (and such a letter as this one) was beyond the
wildest hopes of any experienced Intelligence officer
—a fulfillment of the daydreams of his hopeful
youth. Such information as the letter contained, if
acted upon efficiently by the General Staff, might
avert a disaster, or might result in the infliction of a
crushing defeat on the Allies at a crucial moment in
the war, and thus alter the whole history of the world.

It was for this reason that I had fought so hard
against the suggestions that we should play safe, that
we should use this plan to plant some minor misin-

[1] The Head of German Military Intelligence and Espionage.

formation contained in documents passing between officers of junior rank. If the letters that Major Martin had carried had been of that sort, not only might the Germans not have made the effort to get copies, but even if they had, they might not have relied on them when making strategic decisions. But what Sir Archibald Nye wrote to General Alexander *must* be true; the Vice-Chief of the Imperial General Staff must *know* what the Allied plans were—*he* could not be himself the victim of a "cover plan" or misinformed. If the German Intelligence Service swallowed these letters as genuine, they would have to "go to town" on them—and no General Staff which got such information with its Intelligence Service's imprimatur of genuineness could fail to base its strategy upon it.

So we sat back and waited. D-day of "Operation Husky" came, and the assault went well. Sicily is roughly a triangle standing on its point, and the Allies landed in the early hours of the morning of the 10th July on either side of this point and advanced rapidly up the sides of the triangle as well as across the middle. There were many elements that added to the surprise which was achieved, such as the rough weather and the "moon period" which was chosen, but that surprise certainly did nothing to shake the confidence of our group that we had succeeded with "Operation Mincemeat" and contributed our bit.

As Intelligence reports and documents gradually
filtered in from Sicily, that view was confirmed; there
seemed to be little doubt that the Germans had
switched the effort that they had put into preparing
the defenses of Sicily, away from the south (where
we in fact landed) to the western angle of the triangle and the northern side, which would have been
the danger-points if we had been making a diversionary assault during an invasion of Sardinia, or an
assault after Sardinia had been captured. Not only
were most of the later minefields, demolitions and
defenses built in the north of Sicily, but the total of
defenses and reinforcements in the island was less
than had been expected and surprisingly deficient in
the south and east. On the information that was available, it was decided officially that our part in the deception had been successful. The view formed by
those in authority on the whole operation was
summed up when the Admiral Cunningham reported,
"The very efficient cover plan and the deceptive
routing of convoys played their part" in the surprise achieved—how preponderantly it was due to
the former we were only to know later.

For real knowledge of the extent and degree of
our success did not come until very much later—not,
in fact, until some months after "V.E.-Day."

I was quietly slogging away one morning in my
stuffy and ill-ventilated room in the bowels of the
Admiralty—winding up my work, writing records of

what had been done, for the guidance of those in
future wars who would never have time to read them
(or think them worth reading), and impatiently waiting for the date for the demobilization of my "Group"
to come round—when the telephone bell rang. It
was D.D.N.I.,[1] and his voice was so distorted with
laughter that I found it hard to understand what he
was saying, though I gathered that he wanted me
in his room. So I went up there and, still shaking
with laughter, he pushed some documents across the
table to me. I picked them up and recognized them,
in spite of the fact that the first words that caught
my eye on the upper one were *"Lieber Grossad-
miral"*! They were the "Mincemeat" letters, or at
least the German translations of them, finishing their
long journey!

D.D.N.I. then explained the cause of his laughter.
An officer was in charge of the sorting and translation
of the German naval archives which had been captured at Tambach in Germany. He had come up to
D.D.N.I.'s room that morning with a very worried
face, and had asked for instructions; his report was
as follows:

In the file of documents that he was examining he
had discovered "these two documents": one was a
copy of a most secret letter from the V.C.I.G.S. to
General Alexander and (he said) it looked as if there

[1] Deputy Director of Naval Intelligence.

had been a fearful breach of security, as well as probable breaches of all sorts of regulations; normally, he ought to hand copies of letters of military importance over to his opposite number in the War Office, but this affair seemed to be so "hot" and fraught with high level complications that he felt that D.D.N.I. might like to handle it himself on his level!

D.D.N.I. had recognized the letters and put the officer's mind at rest. There then began a search for other documents bearing on the matter, and we soon found evidence of the completeness of our triumph over the German Intelligence Service.

As we had anticipated, they had immediately recognized the vital importance to their Operational Staff of these documents, if genuine, and had wasted no time.

Their agents in Madrid must have telegraphed the contents of the documents and an account of their discovery to Berlin early in the first week of May, because we have found reference in a later document to the fact that an Intelligence appreciation of Allied intentions had been circulated by signal on the 9th May before the "original documents" had been received in Berlin.

When the German Intelligence Service in Berlin received this information, they had obviously reacted as we expected them to do, and had demanded evidence to support the authenticity of the documents, for the first written report from Madrid had been followed by a second and more detailed one; this latter indicated that still further inquiries would be made. But time was short; Berlin had clearly appreciated the importance of the information and had decided that the details given by Madrid were convincing. And they had indeed, "gone to town" on it!

The first document of importance was an Intelligence appreciation which had been attached to a translation into German of the letter from Sir Archibald Nye to General Alexander. It was dated the 14th May, 1943, and had been stamped with the "most secret" instructions: "To be circulated personally! Not through Registry!" The circulation marked on it was to the Commander-in-Chief of Naval Staff, Admiral Doenitz, and on the 15th May his Chief of Staff had initialled it and marked it with a cross, in blue pencil, to signify that Doenitz should read it himself; this the latter did, obliterating the cross in green pencil with his personal "squiggle" and the figures 18 to indicate the date when he read it on his return to his H.Q. from his visits to Mussolini and Hitler; there were also two other officers included in the circulation.

This document read as follows:

Subject: Captured Enemy Document on Mediterranean Operations.
    Attached herewith are:

(*a*) Translation of the captured letter from the Imperial Staff to General ALEXANDER.

(*b*) Appreciation thereof by the (German) General Staff.

The contents of further captured documents are unimportant. Exhaustive examination by 3 Skl. revealed the following:

1. The genuineness of the captured documents is above suspicion. The suggestion that they have intentionally fallen into our hands—of which the probability is slight —and the question whether the enemy is aware of the capture of the documents by us or only of their loss at sea is being followed up. It is possible that the enemy has no knowledge of the capture of the documents.

Against that it is certain that he knows that they did not reach their destination.

2. Whether the enemy will now alter his intended operations or will set an earlier date for their commencement must be taken into consideration, but seems unlikely.

3. *Probable Date of the Operation*

The matter is being treated as urgent; yet there is still time on the 23rd April to inform General Alexander by air courier of General Wilson's proposal to use Sicily as cover-target for the assault in the Eastern Mediterranean, wherein he is requested to reply immediately in the event of his supporting Wilson's opinion, "as we cannot postpone the matter much longer." In this case the Imperial General Staff considers altering the planning both in the Eastern and Western Mediterranean, for which there is still time.

4. *Sequence of the Operations.*

It is presumed that both operations will take place simultaneously, since Sicily is unsuitable as a cover-target simultaneously for both.

5. The Tobruk area comes into consideration as a starting-point for the operations in the Eastern Mediterranean. Alexandria is not considered, as in this case Sicily would have been absurd as a cover-target.

6. It is not clear whether the deception worked by the cover-target concerns only the period up to the beginning of the operations or whether in fact a cover-operation would be used as well as the actual assault.

7. It is *not* clear from the attached whether *only* the 5th and 56th Divisions will be landed in the Eastern Mediterranean (at Araxos and Kalamata). However *only* these two Divisions are to be reinforced for their assault. It is always possible that all assault troops and targets are included with them.

8. It should be emphasized that it is obvious from this document that big preparations are in course in the Eastern Mediterranean as well. This is important, because considerably less intelligence about preparations has reached us from this area than from Algeria, owing to their geographical situation.

The first point that strikes one is that the German Intelligence Service is already committing itself to the categorical assertion that "The genuineness of the captured documents is above suspicion," and, although they do prudently cover themselves with a reservation that they are inquiring into the possibility of a "plant" and the extent of our knowledge of the fate of the documents, they are already saying that the possibility of the first "is slight." They have also already decided that we would be "unlikely" to change our plans or hasten the date of the assault; anyone with experience of the complexity and detail involved in the planning and launching of large-scale operations would agree with that view at least!

Another point which illustrates how, when one is working a deception of this kind, one has to put oneself into the mind of the enemy and to try to assume *his* degree of general knowledge is the statement in Paragraph 5. The Germans say that Sicily is impossible as a cover target for an operation by troops based on Alexandria—presumably because they consider the distance to be too great. Had it been *our* Staff who read the document, the reaction would have been different: they knew that the distance was not too great and that troops from Alexandria could be used in an assault on Sicily, as, in fact, took place.

I need not consider the rest of the document in detail, as I will deal in the next chapter with the Operational Staffs' appreciations of the documents. But this appreciation does reveal the care with which every word and implication of the V.C.I.G.S.'s letter was studied.

This document was followed by another report circulated by the German Intelligence Service which was dated the 15th May, 1943. It read as follows:

Subject: *British Official Mail Washed Ashore Near Huelva*

The following points were cleared up in a conversation on 10.5.43 with the official concerned, a Spanish staff officer with whom we have been in contact for many years:

1. Clutched in the hand of the corpse was an ordinary briefcase which contained the following documents:

(*a*) A piece of ordinary white paper containing letters addressed to General Alexander and Admiral Cunningham. This white paper bore no writing on it.

Each of the three letters was in a separate envelope with the usual form of address and directed personally to the addressee, sealed apparently with the sender's private seal (signet ring).

The seals were in perfect condition. The letters themselves, which I have had in my hands in their re-sealed envelopes, are in good condition. For reproduction purposes the Spaniards had dried them with artificial heat and then placed them in salt water for twenty-four hours, without greatly altering their condition.

(*b*) Also in the briefcase were the proofs of the pamphlet on the operations of the Combined Operations Command mentioned by Mountbatten in his letter of the 22nd April, as well as the photographs mentioned therein.

The proofs were in perfect condition, but the photographs were quite ruined.

2. The messenger also carried a note-case in the breast pocket of his coat with personal papers, including his military papers with photographs (according to these, he was the Major Martin referred to in Mountbatten's letter of the 22nd April), a letter to Major Martin from his fiancée and one from his father, and a London night-club bill dated the 27th April.

Major Martin therefore left London on the morning of the 28th April, the same day that the aircraft came to grief near Huelva.

3. The British Consul was present at the discovery and is fully informed about it. The expected suggestions by the British Consul that the documents should be handed over to him were set aside under the pretext that all articles found on the body, including all papers, must be laid before the local Spanish magistrate.

After being reproduced, all documents were returned to their original condition by the Spanish General Staff and definitely give the impression—as I was able to see for myself—that they had not been opened. They will be returned to the English today through the Spanish Foreign Office.

Further inquiries are being made by the Spanish General Staff concerning the whereabouts of the pilot of the aircraft, who was presumably injured in the crash, and an interrogation of the latter about any other passengers.

From the point of view of our little group, this was a most fascinating document. It fully justified

the care with which we had built up the personality
of Major Martin, so that the very "reality" of that officer carried conviction as to the genuineness of the
documents that he was carrying, although it does reveal how chance would render some details important and others unimportant. It also reveals how accurate we were in our belief, on which the whole
operation was based, that the Germans would have
complete access to anything that interested them,
once it was placed in the hands of the Spanish Staff.

The first point that emerges is that, as I have already said, we need not have worried whether the
attachment of the briefcase to Major Martin by a
chain was plausible or not as the Germans were told
that he had the briefcase clutched in his hand; so
the inefficiency of the Spaniards, as well as their co-
operation with the Germans, helped us.

I do not follow the reference in Paragraph 1 (*a*) to
a "piece of plain white paper" round the envelopes;
either this was something that some Spaniard put
round them to preserve them from stains or some
paper from the bundle of proofs of the Combined
Operations pamphlet had become misplaced; anyhow,
we had not wrapped up the envelopes. Also the seals
were official seals with the Royal Coat of Arms.

Then we noted that the personal papers in the
wallet had been extracted and inspected, and we
were glad that the letters from Pam and Major Martin's father had not been missed—that artistic effort was

not wasted! Also Lord Louis Mountbatten's letter to
Admiral Cunningham is shown to have played its
intended part in establishing who Major Martin was.

But this report illustrates one of the greatest difficulties that has to be faced in carrying out a deception. The deceiver can only supply his opponent with
the material and has to leave that opponent to draw
the deductions from it: for that reason he has to
gauge both the efficiency and the intelligence with
which his material will be treated. I feel that our
deduction as to the intelligence of the Germans
was about right, but we may have put their efficiency
too high, for they made two extremely careless mis-
takes—both about dates.

As can be seen by a comparison of the photographs
of Lord Louis Mountbatten's letter to Admiral Cunningham and the photostat of the German translation
of the same document (between pages 64 and 65),
the Germans were too careless to copy the date cor-
rectly. The letter was dated 21st April, but the Germans, either in copying the letter or in translating it
into German, altered the date to the 22nd April.

As it happened, that did not matter, but the other
mistake was much more dangerous. There is a reference in the report to "a London night-club bill dated
the 27th April"; we came to the conclusion that that
must be based on a careless reading of the stubs of
the theatre tickets. The invitation to the Cabaret
Club was not only not a bill, but it was not dated

at all. It could not have been the bill dated the 24th
April for his room for several nights at the Naval
and Military Club, since that did not look like a
night-club bill, and surely even the Spaniards would
not have mistaken the "In and Out" for a night-club!
So we came to the conclusion that this error was due
to a careless confusion between the stubs from the
Prince of Wales' Theatre and the invitation to the
Cabaret Club. That did not matter, but the mistake
in the date might have been more serious.

The report decided, as we intended the Germans
to believe, that Major Martin flew from England the
day after he had had his farewell party; but the error
in the date fixed that departure as having taken place
"on the morning of the 28th April, the same day that
the aircraft came to grief near Huelva." Had the Germans considered the opinion of the Spanish doctor, of
which at least their agent in Huelva must have been
aware, as to the date of death, and linked it with this
date of departure, they might have become suspicious. The Spanish doctor had, not unreasonably,
put the date as several days before the body was recovered on the 30th April: the shortest time that was
suggested was some five days. So, on that basis, the
aircraft disaster which caused Major Martin's death
must have taken place on about the 25th April.

I am not sufficient of a philosopher to work out
what can be deduced from this. It could be argued
that we had been lucky that no one noticed this

discrepancy and that our deception ought to have
been "blown." I hope it is not too egotistical to say
that I do not accept that. We had provided the
Spaniards and Germans with all the clues from which
they could draw the deductions that we wanted.
While I suppose it would be absurd to say that we
were entitled to reasonably competent and intelligent co-operation from the other side, I think we can
say that we *had* provided the right clues and that
they *did* draw the right deductions, even if those
deductions were only reached by a cancelling out of
compensating errors!

Anyhow, the report shows that the Germans did
deduce that Major Martin *must* have travelled by air
and that the disaster to the aircraft took place on a
date consistent both with his departure and his state
when he arrived.

The next paragraph of the report also interested
us. It revealed that our view of the efficiency of Ger-
man-Spanish co-operation at Huelva was fully justified. It recorded how, when the fortuitous interven-
tion by a military unit and a naval judicial officer
precluded immediate access to the documents, the
efforts of the British Vice-Consul to take charge of
them were "set aside" under a "pretext." We knew
that we could "trust" the Spaniards!

Finally, there is the record of the fact that the envelopes, with the letters restored to them, and other
papers were not returned until after the German

agent had himself inspected and handled them. That he thought that the letters "gave the impression that they had not been opened" does not surprise me: they would have given me the same impression if we had not taken precautions.

So, as far as the German Intelligence Service was concerned, we had won; as far as they were concerned, one could repeat the view of the Chiefs of Staff, as regards the Spaniards, "Mincemeat Swallowed Whole." The Intelligence Service, at any rate, had accepted the whole thing as genuine. But, as I have indicated before, that would have been only a hollow victory if the German Operational Staff had failed to take the same view and had continued to go all out in preparing to meet an invasion of Sicily. But they swallowed it also, and they also "went to town."

13.

THE GERMAN HIGH COMMAND GETS BUSY

THE INFORMATION that we gleaned from the German naval archives captured at Tambach was equally revealing with regard to the reactions that "Operation Mincemeat" produced from the German High Command. The results that we gained were far beyond our wildest hopes.

Our guess as to what the Germans originally thought the Allies were going to do after Tunisia had fallen had been right, and we had even underestimated the difficulties that we were up against. We found a copy of a message sent by the German High Command to their army in Tunisia in February of 1943. They had decided that our next operation would be in the Mediterranean, and that it would be against one of the large islands; they put the order

of probability as Sicily first, with Crete second and
Sardinia and Corsica following behind. So, when we
were doing our planning in London we were right
in thinking that, from a very early stage, the Germans would put Sicily at the head of the betting, and
as our preparations grew in the western Mediterranean they would have realized that *those* could
not be for an assault on Crete, with an un-reduced
Sicily barring the way. We had guessed right about
that, but the message included the statement "from
reports coming in about Anglo-American landing intentions it is apparent that the enemy is practicing
deception on a large scale." They were going to turn
out to be accurate about that also, but had the Chiefs
of Staff known how alert the Germans were for deception, I wonder whether we ever *would* have got permission to launch "Mincemeat"!

The documents reveal that this strategic appreciation was maintained right up to the beginning of
May, 1943. And then, on the 9th May, the whole picture changed: the news of the capture of Major
Martin's documents had reached the High Command.

On the 9th May an Intelligence appreciation must
have reached the High Command, for we found the
following document in the file just after the appreciation dated the 14th May mentioned in the last chapter:

Further to my 2144/43 dated 9.5.43, following appreciation has been made on receipt of original material:

1. A landing in the eastern and western Mediterranean on a fairly large scale is anticipated.

(*a*) Target of the operation in eastern Mediterranean under General Wilson is the coast near Kalamata and the stretch of coast south of Cape Araxos (both on the West coast of the Peloponnese). The reinforced 56th Infantry Division is detailed for the landing at Kalamata and the reinforced 5th Infantry Division at Cape Araxos. It is not known whether both divisions will land in force or in part only. In the first instance, a lapse of at least 2–3 weeks would be required as the 56th Division on 9.5.43 was engaged at Enfidaville with two brigades and must first be rested and embarked. This solution, which embraces a certain delay before the landing can take place, appears to be the more probable from the way in which the letter is written. However, if the landing is to be effected by only certain units of both divisions, it could be made at any time, as one brigade of the 56th Division and 1–2 brigades of the 5th Division are probably already available in the actual starting-area (Egypt-Libya). Code-name for the landing on the Peloponnese is "HUSKY." The Anglo-American General Staff has proposed a simultaneous cover operation against the Dodecanese to General Wilson. Wilson's decision thereon was not yet taken on 23.4.43.

(*b*) Target for the operation under General Alexander in the western Mediterranean is not mentioned. A joking reference in the letter points to Sardinia. Code-name for this operation is "BRIMSTONE." The proposed cover target for operation "BRIMSTONE" is Sicily.

2. Maintenance of completest secrecy over this discovery and utmost limitation of circulation of this information is essential.

On a point of detail, this document gave me great
pleasure. I had already congratulated myself that
the German agent in Madrid had bothered to send on
a copy of the seemingly unimportant letter from Lord
Louis Mountbatten to Admiral Cunningham, unlike
his treatment of the equally unimportant letter to
General Eisenhower. *Was* it because of the hint that
we thought we had failed at Dieppe? But Paragraph
1· (*b*) of this appreciation showed that my heavy-
footed joke about sardines had gone home—"a joking reference in the letter points to Sardinia"; it was
not the same letter, but that can be excused in an
appreciation of this kind. The German sense of
humor is a great asset.

The German Intelligence Service had swallowed
the deception: now the High Command accepted
this view. It may well be that we have Hitler to thank
for this, for we know, from the diary of Admiral
Doenitz's conferences with the Fuehrer, that by the
14th May Hitler was convinced of the · genuineness
of the documents, and what they foretold. For
Doenitz had been sent to Italy to try to stiffen Mussolini after the North African disasters, and he reported to Hitler on his way back to his own headquarters before he himself had seen the documents;

in reply to a question by Hitler as to Mussolini's views on "Anglo-American intentions," he reported that the Duce was convinced that we would attack Sicily; and here is his record of Hitler's reply:

The Fuehrer does not agree with the Duce that the most likely invasion point is Sicily. Furthermore, he believes that the discovered Anglo-Saxon order confirms the assumption that the planned attack will be directed mainly against Sardinia and the Peloponnesus.

It is clear that Hitler was completely sold on the idea that we were intending to land in Greece and, now that he had come to this conclusion, he stuck firmly to it. So much so that, on the 23rd July, nearly a fortnight after the Allied landing in Sicily, Hitler *still* believed that the main operation was going to be an invasion of Greece, and appointed his favorite general, General Rommel, to command the forces that were being assembled there. On the 25th July Rommel flew to Greece, whence he had to be hurriedly recalled to take over the command in Italy and rally the defense of that country after the fall of Mussolini.

But it would be unfair to put too much blame on Hitler. On the very same day that Hitler had corrected the Duce's opinion, the 14th May, the Official War Diary of the German Naval High Command recorded the fact that the General Staff of the Army had come to the definite conclusion that the documents were genuine; they concluded that the assault would be on Sardinia, but that there might be a diversionary attack on Sicily.

So, by the 14th May, 1943, the Operational Staffs, the Supreme Command and the Fuehrer himself were all convinced. "Operation Mincemeat" was completely successful. It remained for us to discover just what this eventually meant to the "Anglo-American" forces.

I do not know in any detail what the German Army and the Luftwaffe were doing, but that they were doing something considerable is evidenced by an order sending the 1st German Panzer Division all the way across Europe from France to establish its headquarters at Tripolis, a town in the Peloponnesus ideally situated to command resistance against landings which included Kalamata and Araxos. When one considers the enormous effort involved in a journey of this kind for a complete Panzer Division, and how it put that force "out of the war" for the time being, one might say that that alone would have far more than repaid the effort that we put into "Operation Mincemeat," even if we had not assisted the invasion of Sicily at all.

We also found in the German records a memorandum of the fact that the German Foreign Office had been asked to warn the Turkish Government that troops and shipping were being moved to Greece, but to stress that there were no hostile intentions against Turkey.

This precaution was not surprising when we consider the extent of the German preparations, for, although, as I have said, I have no details of the Army and Luftwaffe movements and activities, they may well have been large if we judge by the German naval activity, of which we naturally found a much more detailed picture among these documents.

By the 20th May the Naval High Command had ordered [1] the laying or the completion of three new German minefields off Greece, including one off Kalamata itself. The German Admiral commanding in the Ægean was ordered to take over control of minefields that the Italians were laying off the western coast of Greece, and German coastal-defense batteries were to be set up in territory under Italian control. These were only some of the steps that were "envisaged or have already been taken" by that date as the Germans had appreciated that almost the whole coast of Greece, as well as the Greek islands, was threatened, though it was hoped that the Allied assaults might be beaten off in spite of German weakness in that area.

These instructions were completed by orders to

[1] See Appendix I.

establish R-boat[2] bases, command stations, naval
sea patrol services and other safeguards: the effort
to be put in was intense.

The dividend from "Mincemeat" was growing, and
that it was a dividend from "Mincemeat" alone is
established by documents which show that these
orders were based on Major Martin's letters (a point
that would have to be concealed in the operational
orders themselves for reasons of security). Another
indication is given by the statement in the orders
that the likelihood of a large scale Allied landing
in the eastern as well as the western Mediterranean
had been established in spite of the fact that "so
far indications of the preparation of large numbers
of landing craft have reached us only from the Western Mediterranean"; in addition, it is possible for
those who compare both documents—the "Mincemeat" letter and these orders—to trace the connection.

Shortly after this, in early June, a whole group of
German R-boats was sent *from* Sicily *to* the Ægean!
Our dividend was indeed growing fast.

Meanwhile, things were moving in the western
Mediterranean area also. I can summarize the main
reaction best by reference to an order sent out on
the 14th June in Hitler's name by General Keitel,
Commander-in-Chief of the Supreme Command of

[2] German Motor Torpedo Boats.

the German Armed Forces. These orders [3] are clearly based on the German appreciation that the use of Sicily as a "cover target" for the assault on Sardinia might involve a diversionary attack on that island (they took a similar view of our use of the Dodecanese as a cover target for the eastern Mediterranean operation: see Appendix I and the appreciation of the 14th May). The operation of that factor on the mind of the German Staff is evidenced also by the location of the German defensive measures which we found in Sicily, as I have already recorded.

We also found a record of the fact that a strong Panzer force with its ancillaries and supplies for for two months was sent to Corsica in June by an order issued in Hitler's name, and from now on there was a growing emphasis on the reinforcement of Sardinia and Corsica, with the north coast of Sicily coming next in priority.

On the 9th July, *the day before we landed in Sicily*, Keitel sent out a long appreciation which he says is that of Doenitz. This appreciation covered not only both the eastern and western Mediterranean, but also future Allied strategy based on operations in both those areas; in it he concludes that an attack on all three islands, Corsica, Sardinia and Sicily (either all together or one at a time), as well

[3] Appendix II.

as the Greek operation, is possible. Doenitz estimates
that there are enough Allied troops in the whole of
North Africa to provide for both operations and
then to exploit the bridgehead that the Allies may
be able to form in Greece; his appreciation is that
a major landing on the coast of Italy (after the capture of the Italian islands) is unlikely, as the Germans could react fast in Italy, whereas in Greece
their reinforcements and supplies would necessarily
be slow, and from Greece the Allies could attack
the Rumanian oilfields, and the political effect of
such an operation on Hungary, as well as Rumania,
might be great. Finally, Doenitz's conclusion, pro-
mulgated by Keitel, is that "the western assault
forces appear to be ready for an immediate attack,"
which could begin at any time (how right he was!),
whereas "the eastern force appears still to be forming up" (how wrong he was: they in fact took part
in the invasion of Sicily).

On the early morning of the 10th July our forces
had landed in Sicily, but the Germans still could not
believe that that was the real assault (and that the
documents must have been a plant): the German
High Command asked that a special look-out should
be kept by the German agents on the shores of the
Straits of Gibraltar for convoys which would be
going to attack Corsica and Sardinia—they presumably still thought that the landings in Sicily (although on the side of the island that they did not

anticipate) were a diversion to draw attention from the main operation.

But by the 12th July even the German belief in the accuracy of the "Mincemeat" documents had begun to weaken—after all, the invasion of Sicily was obviously genuine and had been going on for two days.

We found two messages passing between the German Naval Commander-in-Chief in Italy and the Naval High Command. In the first, the Commander-in-Chief complains bitterly that the departure of the 1st R-Boat Group (which had been sent to the Ægean for the defense of Greece) had prejudiced the defense of Sicily, as a gap had been left in the patrols, which were consequently ineffective. He stated that the shortage of small craft was "chronic" and that the departure of any more boats, as ordered, would have a serious effect both on defensive work and on escort work. The reply stated that reconnaissance reports had shown the Allies to have engaged so much in Sicily that there was little probability of landings in Greece until the Sicilian operation was over; the defense of Greece could take second place "for the time being" (was "Mincemeat" *still* having some influence on the High Command as well as on Hitler?), and the order for seven boats of the 11th R-boat Flotilla to go to the Ægean was cancelled: these boats could remain under the orders of the Commander-in-Chief, Italy.

So the immediate repercussions of "Operation Mincemeat" had finally ended—except, for the German forces still sitting idle in Greece. The survey that has been made of its results can be summarized as follows:

As regards the working out of the "Operation": we fooled those of the Spaniards who assisted the Germans; we fooled the German Intelligence Service both in Spain and in Berlin; we fooled the German Operational Staff and Supreme Command; we fooled Keitel; and, finally, we fooled Hitler himself, and kept him fooled right up to the end of July.

As regards the eastern Mediterranean: we caused immense effort to be put into the defense of Greece, with the creation of minefields, shore batteries, etc.; we caused a concentration of troops in Greece which justified the appointment by Hitler of Rommel to command them; these troops included a Panzer Division which had to be sent right across Europe; all this was completely wasted effort from the German point of view and diminished the potential defense of Sicily and of Italy.

As regards the western Mediterranean: we caused an increase in the fortification and reinforcement of Corsica and Sardinia at the expense of that of Sicily; we caused the defensive preparations in Sicily to be largely diverted from those coasts of the island where the Allies in fact landed to the coasts where they did not land; we caused the Germans to send R-boats away from Sicily to the Ægean, thus opening a gap in their defenses which "prejudiced the defense of Sicily" as well as creating a shortage of escort vessels.

All this can be traced from the contemporary documents, and I think that I can fairly claim that our dividends from the "Operation" were indeed enormous—far greater than we had anticipated in even our most sanguine moments. It is for others to assess how many British and American lives were saved by "The Man Who Never Was" during the conquest of Sicily, and what effect his exploit had on the course of the war.

ENVOI

RATHER THAN CONCLUDE on a somewhat bombastic
note—a note that I feel to be owed to the mem-
ory of the man who really was, and who became
"Major Martin, Royal Marines"—I would like to add
something that puts my own part in the "Operation"
into its proper perspective.

As the result of what we already knew of the success of "Operation Mincemeat," I was awarded the
Military O.B.E. in 1944. When he was pinning the
medal on to my uniform jacket, His Majesty asked
me where it was that I had earned it, and on my
replying, "At the Admiralty, Sir," I could see his
eyebrows go up in some astonishment. He followed
with another question: "What did you get it for?"

Taken by surprise, I could only ejaculate: "Part of the planning of 'Operation Husky,' Sir."

That reply of mine made me realize how the entire thing fitted together and, as I have said, put the whole picture into its proper perspective. "Operation Mincemeat," with all its thrill and "glamor," was just an integral part of the planning of a modern operation.

APPENDIX
I

Copy of 1st Naval War Staff 1 Ops. 1942/43, Most Secret, S.O. only, of May 20.43

From a teleprinted signal (outgoing) to:
Supreme Command of the Armed Forces/Operations Staff of the Armed Forces.
Copy to: Naval Group Command South, C.-in-C. G.A.F., Operations Staff of the G.A.F. 1a (Naval), Captain Mossel, Supreme Command of the Army/Army General Staff Naval Liaison Officer, Captain Weygoldt.
Cleared as Single Address Message.
Most Secret for S.O. only.

The Naval War Staff has examined exhaustively the possibilities of enemy landing operation in the

Southeastern Area and has come to the following conclusions:

(1) (*i*) The possibility of enemy landings in the Eastern as well as the Western Mediterranean must be reckoned with although reliable evidence about the preparation of a large number of landing craft is so far available from the W. Med. only.

(*ii*) Possible starting-points for landing operations:

(*a*) ARTA-PYRGOS area: Gulf of Arta, Gulf of Patras, the coast South of Cape Araxos and on both sides of Pyrgos and also islands off these areas, especially Corfu and Cephalonia.

(*b*) The South coats of the Peloponnese: Navarino, Gulf of Corone (Kalamata) and Gulf of Marathon.

(*c*) CRETE: Preferably the North coast, on the South coast Mesara Bay and Hierapetra, but only with limited forces.

(*d*) RHODES.

(*e*) Islands in the AEGEAN: Leros, Milos, Chios, Mytilene and Lemnos.

(*f*) The East coast of the PELOPONNESE and Central GREECE: Gulf of Nauplia, Gulf of Petali (East coast of Attica).

(*g*) SALONICA: Gulf of Salonica, Gulf of Orphani.

(*h*) THRACE: Gulf of Cavalla and the coast to the East of Thasos.

(*iii*) It can be assumed that the enemy will probably make an initial landing where he believes there will be the least resistance and where he expects the greatest results in the shortest time. Therefore an initial landing on CRETE can be ruled out for the moment; in view of the advanced state of the development and equipment of the Fortress of CRETE a very considerable expenditure of strength would be required and a prerequisite would be subsidiary operations to obtain airfields in the Dodecanese and Peloponnese close to the scene of operations. Further, the capture of CRETE would only represent a partial accomplishment of his aims. A thrust past CRETE into the AEGEAN, the occupation of the most important islands and a landing attempt on the East coast of the PELOPONNESE and Central GREECE is likewise improbable. An attempt at an immediate thrust into the area of SALONICA and THRACE need not be reckoned with. For such operations the enemy would require very large forces to protect his supply-routes. Considerable losses would be unavoidable as long as German air and light Naval forces (S-boats) can be operated from CRETE.

(*iv*) In the opinion of the Naval War Staff landing attempts are most likely to be made in the Greek West coast area - where the CORFU-ARTA-PYRGOS region offers the greatest prospects of success.

Possibilities: a thrust from the North towards LARISSA-VOLOS, cutting off Central GREECE with the PELOPONNESE; in the center an advance towards Central GREECE and ATTICA. In the South a drive for the CORINTH Isthmus. The islands off this coast (especially CORFU and CEPHALONIA) would become very valuable bases in enemy hands. Special attention is drawn to the exceptional importance of these islands.

Simultaneous subsidiary landings are probable at NAVARINO (a good harbor for Naval forces operating for the protection of landings and supplies), KALAMATA (airfield) and perhaps also the Gulf of MARATHON. A subsidiary thrust through TRIPOLIS to CORINTH. Simultaneously or shortly beforehand a diversionary operation against the DODECANESE (RHODES) is to be expected.

(2) The defensive power of the areas in the greatest danger is still weak. Nevertheless in the opinion of the Naval War Staff it should be possible to throw back attempted enemy landings if he attacks with only limited forces. According to evidence from the Army General Staff available to Naval War Staff the enemy has at present only a few divisions available in the E. Med. Also the available transport space is sufficient for these forces only.

All measures must therefore be taken to reinforce rapidly the defensive strength of the areas which are specially threatened. The construction of a secondary line of defense in the rear (roughly in the N. GREECE-SALONICA area) is only to be considered when the other has been accomplished.

(3) The following immediate steps are envisaged or have already been taken by the Naval War Staff:

(i) Laying of German minefields: off KALAMATA in the process of completion, CERIGO Strait complete,

CERIGOTTO Strait in preparation. Group Command South (Admiral Ægean) to exert his influence for the laying of mines by the Italians on the West coast of GREECE.

(*ii*) The installation of coastal batteries, also in the Italian-occupied area (the decision of the Supreme Commander of the Armed Forces has been requested).

(*iii*) PIRAEUS and SALONICA are intended as the principal bases for Naval forces and are or will be appropriately supplied. MELOS, LEROS and LEMNOS as auxiliary bases will receive only limited supplies for Naval forces.

(*iv*) The possibility of installing operational bases for S-boats on the PELOPONNESE and CRETE is being explored.

(*v*) Preliminary discussion with C.-and-C. G.A.F. South East concerning reconnaissance and offensive action by the G.A.F. after the approach of enemy operations has been established (air attacks on the landing fleet where possible while it is still in its port of departure and mining these harbors from the air):

(*vi*) Preparation of a patrol-service with coastal defense vessels to the West, South and East of CRETE.

(*vii*) Preparation of a Command Station for Admiral Ægean at SALONICA to ensure uninterrupted control in the event of it proving necessary to move the headquarters.

Naval War Staff Reg. No. 1st Naval War Staff 1 Op. 1492/43. Most Secret. S.O. only.

APPENDIX II

Reg. No. Naval War Staff 1 17 189/43. Most Secret.
Distribution: Copy No. 1. Chief Naval War Staff
         2. Naval War Staff
         3. 1a
         4. 1 ops
         5. 1 m
         6. Naval War Staff qu A
         7.   " " " " "
         8. 1 f
         9. 1 b
         File 13.

Teleprint MBBZ 02175 of 14.6.43 23.34.
Most immediate GWASL 02633 14.6 2130.
To Supreme Command of the Navy, Naval War
  Staff.
Also for: General Staff of the Army, Inspector-Gen-

eral of Armored Troops, Supreme Command of
the Navy (Naval War Staff, C.-in-C. South, Home
Staff, Overseas Branch).

MOST SECRET

(A) The FUEHRER has issued the following orders
for the reinforcement of SARDINIA and SICILY.

(1) Measures to be taken by the Army General
Staff:

(*i*) Every island to be provided with a Fortress Infantry Regiment to the strength of one regimental
staff with an H.Q. Coy. and 4 battalions.—3 March
Battalions of the June draft to ITALY may be used if
necessary. In this connection the FUEHRER stressed
especially the need to be strongly equipped with local
weapons suitable for defence against armor and
land attack. For this purpose recourse can even be
had to French 2.5 and 3.7 centimeter anti-tank guns
with stick grenades.

The regiments must be ready to move by 28.6.43.
If it is not possible to procure the anti-tank guns
needed for SICILY by this time the remaining anti-
tank guns must be sent on by 20.7 at the latest.

(*ii*) SARDINIA to be provided with a Fortress Artillery Abteilung for coastal defence.

Equipment—2 batteries of 17-cm. guns.

1 battery of 10-cm. guns

(The latter are available from C.-in-C. South.)

To be prepared to depart as soon as possible.

(*iii*) The SARDINIA detachment to be provided

with 1 anti-tank coy. with 12 anti-tank guns for each regiment.

Every lorried infantry coy. of the SICILY detachment to be equipped with 2 anti-tank guns. If heavy and medium anti-tank guns are not at first available, recourse must be had to light anti-tank guns firing stick grenades. The anti-tank coys. should however be equipped with heavy and medium anti-tank guns.

(*iv*) The SARDINIA Armored Coy. to be expanded to an armored Abteilung with at least 50 tanks (of which at least 25 will be Mark IV) by supplying the necessary units and weapons. To be prepared to move off as soon as possible.

(*v*) The setting up of an armored coy. of 20 tanks Mark IV for the 215th Armored Abteilung in SICILY. (This coy. to be transferred to compensate for the Tiger coy. which was handed over to the Hermann Goering Division.) To be prepared to move off by 15.7.43.

(*vi*) Several W/T detachments to reinforce the Signals Coy. of the SARDINIA Command.

(2) The Supreme Command of the Navy is to form a coastal artillery Abteilung from 3 newly-commissioned batteries and is to transfer them to C.-in-C. South for despatch to SICILY on call.

(3) C.-in-C. South's other requirements must be given lower priority unless a special order to the contrary is given.

(B) (1) The Army General Staff will report to the

Supreme Command of the Allied Forces/Operations
Staff of the Armed Forces:

(*i*) The proposed equipment of the Fortress Regiments with anti-tank guns (statement of calibre)
and other heavy weapons (including rifle-grenade
apparatus).

(*ii*) Details of the distribution of the anti-tank
guns according to caliber amongst the other newly-
created units and reinforcements required.

(*iii*) The times at which the individual reinforcements will be ready to move off (to be reported also
to Home Staff [Overseas Branch]).

(2) The Supreme Command of the Armed Forces
will report to Operations Staff of the Armed Forces
and Home Staff (Overseas Branch) when the coastal
artillery Abteilungen are ready to move off.

(3) Home Staff (Overseas Branch) will be responsible for the rapid passage of these reinforcements.

(*Signed*) KEITEL,

Supreme Command of Armed Forces/
Operations Staff of the Armed Forces.
Op. No. 002820. Most Secret.